2009 Poetry Competition

I have a dream 2009

Words to change the world

Martin Luther King

John Lennon

London

Edited by Vivien Linton

First published in Great Britain in 2009 by:

 Young**Writers**

Young Writers
Remus House
Coltsfoot Drive
Peterborough
PE2 9JX
Telephone: 01733 890066
Website: www.youngwriters.co.uk

Foreword

'I Have a Dream 2009' is a series of poetry collections written by 11 to 18-year-olds from schools and colleges across the UK and overseas. Pupils were invited to send us their poems using the theme 'I Have a Dream'. Selected entries range from dreams they've experienced to childhood fantasies of stardom and wealth, through inspirational poems of their dreams for a better future and of people who have influenced and inspired their lives.

The series is a snapshot of who and what inspires, influences and enthuses young adults of today. It shows an insight into their hopes, dreams and aspirations of the future and displays how their dreams are an escape from the pressures of today's modern life. Young Writers are proud to present this anthology, which is truly inspired and sure to be an inspiration to all who read it.

Contents

The Poems

My Dream: People Taking Things For Granted

Do you take things for granted?
When you're at home in front of the tele?
Watching Big Brother and eating your dinner.

Do you give a second's thought
When you're buying a pair of ugg boots
How people are less fortunate and some have no money at all?

When you're buying a new mountain bike,
To lose weight or just for fun,
While people on the other side are screaming, crying and dying.

On the other side there are wars,
Where children become soldiers
While you're at home, on your phone not caring at all.

On the other side, people walk for miles for one bucket of water
When you can walk 20 seconds where you can get 3 gallons.

The comparison of us and them is very different indeed.

When we're happy, they're distraught,
When we're rich, they are poor,
When we're well fed and they go hungry,
When our health is healthy and theirs is not,
When we can read and write, but they can't a lot.

When we're with our friends in a shopping mall,
They're working for their families,
When we're spending our money in sweet shops,
They're paying doctors to help them survive,
And when it's too late, it's not at all good
Because, when we're living they . . . just . . . die . . .

So now ask yourself a question and be honest with yourself;
Are you taking things for granted?

Betul Koc (13)
Camden School for Girls

1

I Have A Dream

She stands there beside me
Her eyes big on her thin face
Her tear-stained cheeks
Her ragged clothes

Her eyes are beautiful, yet
Sorrowful and deep
They hold many secrets
Never to leave her lips.

Her eyes are too old
For her young body,
They have seen a lot, too much
She has lived through too much.

Suddenly she collapses
Her hands on her ears
She screams and she cries
I feel her pain.

But I stand there beside her
And turn a blind eye
I cannot help her,
She's already died.

Everyone, in their lifetime
Must make a choice
Of whether to help her live
Or let her die.

Should it be so?
Should we have this choice?
Should we be so lucky
To be the ones who decide?

We can't imagine
What went through her mind
As she fell to the floor
As she shouted and cried.

The drill of the machine gun
Her family's shouts
Her mother's screams

As they shot her down.

All I can wish for
Is everyone who can
Will give at least something
To people like her.

Tasha Pick (13)
Camden School for Girls

Wishes

Far off in the future
When birds may not even fly
My dreams might come true
Just listen and please don't cry

I may only be young
But I still do have a dream
That anyone can give a thought
That being healthy includes ice cream

I wish that when I'm older
I can hold my head up high
People aren't just colours
They are people who pass me by

Anyone can have wishes
It doesn't matter if you're big or small
I know I have more than one
I won't have time to say them all

Life isn't just about taking
It's always about giving too
When you really care for someone
They'll think of giving that love back to you

Look all around you
And think of what you're seeing
Don't think too much of what you want
Just be glad to be a human being.

Maya Sarch Thomas (12)
Camden School for Girls

A Speck Of Dust In A Giant's Eye

We are humans with a rhythm for life,
A speck of dust in a giant's eye,
The world is big and we are small,
All we've got to do is just ask, 'Why?'

'Why does that man beat that boy?'
'Why do they treat those girls as toys?'
'Why does the world keep spinning so
When people are suffering and we are too slow?'

To change the law, we have to break it,
To survive in life, we have to make it,
To help the world, we have to save it,
To make them listen we have to fake it.

Survivors take liberties,
Survivors hold on,
Survivors like them
Just shine like the sun.

Equality is crucial,
Just open your eyes
To the suffering of the world,
Before they all die.

We need to lose ourselves to be found,
Don't ignore the cries, the shouts, the sound.

She hears the footsteps,
Pounding fast,
She holds her breathing
As they run past.

It's an accident of birth,
But we *can* help it.
It's an accident of birth,
But we *can* save them.

Lola Karpf (13)
Camden School for Girls

4

I Have A Dream

I have a dream
That I can walk along the street with no fear,
That I can say my political views without any bad consequences,
That we will live in a conflict free world,
I have a dream.

I have a dream,
That my dad is superman,
That girls won't be so mean,
That my teachers will hand out chocolate, not homework,
I have a dream.

I have a dream
That children can play in the park after 5 o'clock,
That mobile phones are for texting, rather than safety,
That the loudest voice will come from the smallest person,
I have a dream.

I have a dream,
That boys won't be monsters,
That my parents won't be embarrassing,
That my friends won't gossip,
I have a dream.

I have a dream
That all children will have a chance to shine,
That racism will be a thing of the past,
That everyone around the world will be equal,
I have a dream,
I have a dream,
I have a dream.

Clara McDade (11)
Camden School for Girls

Change

Make history,
Help the world,
Open doors,
Imagine.

Trust decisions,
Be your own person,
Reach into people's minds,
Let your ideas discover a voice,
Believe in yourself,
Inspire.

Encounter whatever touches your heart,
Follow where the journey takes you,
Don't be afraid to risk,
Always be able,
Always be strong,
Sacrifice.

Be a leader not a follower,
Take on the world,
Dreams are a few steps away,
Be independent,
It just takes motivation and determination,
Explore.

Achieve your goals.
Work hard for your life,
Your future is in your hands,
One day - change will come.

Kamara Simms (12)
Camden School for Girls

I Have A Dream

Last night I had a dream,
That the world did not really seem
As nasty as it really is,
I dreamt we all lived in bliss.

I dreamt that people would not dare
To hurt people without a care,
The world was filled with endless joy,
Everything connecting; like a child with a toy.

The weather was good, the sky was blue,
Nobody was sick with the flu,
The adults had a chance to rest,
Everyone was at their best.

Last night I had a dream,
That everything was as charming as whipped cream,
In my dream I changed the universe,
I broke the Earth's unbreakable curse.

The world lived in peace and harmony,
And everybody acted very, very calmly,
I knew this dream was too good to be true,
Because people always harm the world, people do.

The next morning, I went out there,
To show some people that I really do care.
You don't have to be famous; you don't need your hair curled,
To be people like me, and change the world.

Sarah Venning (11)
Camden School for Girls

The Great Play

We are all players,
We step onto the stage of life.
We have no lines,
No safe path to pursue,
Not even a plot,
No basic guidelines to follow.
We improvise to begin,
Taking the first shaky steps into a private spotlight
That only you can see.
Then, in what could seem a lifetime,
Or the flutter of a second,
You find *it*.
Your dream.
The climax of the play
And the only barrier,
Thin as paper, yet thick as stone,
Is prejudice and a closed mind
And there is only one way to unveil the dream,
One tool that is a thousand miles away,
Yet buried in your heart,
It is courage.
And when this absurd play is over,
You shall receive applause,
Then a resonant silence,
For there is no more difficult yet rewarding play to perform
Than life.

Julia Lawson (12)
Camden School for Girls

A Broken Home

He sits there waiting, the clock's ticking, 'It's nearly 8!'
The boy keeps thinking, thinking what to do,
What to say, where to go, where to stay -

How to face his dad that day.

A rumble tumble breaks the silence,
But no one knows he won't receive a single penny
To feed his son

The one who sits alone, the one that's scared and frightened,
The one with bruises from his head to toe.

He can't get help, no one knows,

He can't run away, he's tried that before, no money no food,
How long can he live for?
Well at home it's just as hardcore,
He's gone for a day without food at one time,
His dad spent the money on the beer and the wine.

What about Mum? She left when he was four,
He remembers them shouting and she'd walked out the door.

So as the day goes by,
We wonder how much longer he'll stay alive.

And when he goes to bed tonight he's hungry and he's scared,
He'll lay down frightened and maybe he'll dream, just like me.

There'll be an end to child cruelty.

Edith Ault (13)
Camden School for Girls

I Have A Dream

How come some people live the good life
While others have to beg for food?
We sit here in our air-conditioned classrooms
Learning to read, write and otherwise.
Kids out there don't!
Those kids have to work
Collecting water, grinding wheat, never time for play
That feeling of freedom and joy.
So when you're sitting on your comfy sofa
Sipping juice and watching TV
Think of those less fortunate
You might think, what can you do to help?
What can you do to help?
You could collect money for charities
That try to make a change
That change could be giving money
To supply a child with an education
To help them change their future
Give them money to move them out
To a better place for living
Help them with medicine to keep them alive
There is so much you can do
Give something and get something back
Save a life or improve one
Make the world a better place.

Kira Grant (13)
Camden School for Girls

Imagine

Clouds of dust surround her, clogging her streaming eyes,
Agony is everywhere, but she can't feel it,
Which is worse, she asks herself, the horrific pain,
Or this eternal empty hole where her heart was?
Empty.

Bang! Bullets come thick and fast,
Will this roaring ever stop?
Her throat dry, she tries to scream,
Her bottle falls to the floor,
Empty.

Here I sit, surrounded by friends and memories,
Family and possessions, a perfect life,
Trying to imagine the extent of her pain,
Why is it she, and not I? Luck, fate, destiny.
Empty.

Prejudice achieves nothing
Except creating more hate,
If everyone is equal,
Then why can't someone help her?

Empty words,
Empty promises,
Better than an empty heart,
Better than a dying soul.

Anna Pick (13)
Camden School for Girls

11

Having A Dream

I have a dream about the poor people in Africa and India,
People all over the world who have nothing,
Compared to what we have.
The people who live in homes made of mud,
Working all day long.
The people waiting and wondering
If they'll ever get any food ever again.
The people not knowing whether they're getting fresh water
Coming to them ever again.

We sit back at home lying on our luxurious sofas
Waiting for dinner to be made,
Throwing away the leftovers we don't want,
We have fresh water to drink whenever we feel like it
And warm clothes to put on when we go out,
Then we lie back in our lovely comfy beds
Snuggling down to go to sleep
Whilst the people far, far away from us
Have to sleep on hard floors with hardly any clothing.

I have a dream that those people with nothing
Will have what they want.
It's good we do all we can to help those people,
But I wish we could do more.

Alexandra Eastman (13)
Camden School for Girls

I Have A Dream

I have a dream,
To make people have flying power,
So we don't have to waste money on aeroplanes!
I have a dream
To be taller,
So people won't call me a shrimp.
I have a dream
To be more creative,
Because this will help me to achieve my dream.
I have a dream,
To make everyone happy,
So I can't hear others crying.
I have a dream,
To stop selling drugs,
This way no one will die for them.
I have a dream,
To make everyone recycle.
But what can I do with a small body?
All I can do is look.
I have a dream,
Always a dream.

Hoki Leung
Camden School for Girls

I Have A Dream . . .

I have a dream to change the world
To stop war and to stop suffering
To change the way the people think
About the world and the people in it

My dream has come true
I've stopped war and stopped suffering
I've changed the way the people think
About the world and the people in it

Anisa Osman
Camden School for Girls

13

Change

Change is everywhere, for everyone change is there each day,
Each action we take, each action we do, we change our world,
By coming together we can make this place we call home
A much better place.

A moment of change is a powerful thing, each wrong is
Made right and each righting is written down for our children for the future,
to fall back onto and understand the change
Of our lifetime.

Each day we get stronger, our world's powerful, our actions
Less violent, less fierce, less dangerous for us to love and live.

Saying 'no' is a change, saying 'yes' is a change from what
We would have always said years ago, days ago, hours ago.
The understanding of change is working together,
Being together, school changes you too.

Be a better or worse person, you are making a difference
On your life and everyone else's by your actions.
We know what's right, we know what's wrong,
But we carry on, we are scared
Of change, we are prepared for change. We are change.

Amber Marsh-Bailey (13)
Camden School for Girls

My Dream

M y dream is to one day change the world
Y ou *can stop* crime

D reams *can* become reality
R acism *can stop* and *will stop!*
E verything is possible!
A s Martin Luther King said, 'I have a dream.'
M *y dream is to change the world!*

Elouisa Hill (12)
Camden School for Girls

Dream

If I had a dream, I'd dream of a bird
A bird that'd fly
Higher than high, in the sky
I'd rest the bad, and praise the good
I'd fly over
Not knowing I could
At first the terrible sights
The screams and bright, blinding lights
Oh, the terrible sights such as
Bad crowds and extreme fights
But soon I'd know
Petrol and fuels would be in need as such a tool
But this world would have to change
People would daze, and change without rage
All the pain would disappear in just one stage
Life could change, but it has to be made.
And then again I'm just a bird
That no one has seen or heard
Life could change, but it has to be made.

Alexandra Photiou (13)
Camden School for Girls

My Dream

One day I'm going to change the world
One day I'm going to win the Olympics
One day I'm going to end world hunger
One day I'm going to reunite the world
One day I'm going to give equality to all

I've changed the world
I've won the Olympics
I've ended world hunger
I've united the world
Now everyone is equal.

Zahra Suleiman (13)
Camden School for Girls

15

Political Immunity

Our world has suffered, we're only just pulling through,
Why don't we try together for political immunity?

Is it right that some people have nothing
While people take it all?
We know in our heart that it might not last,
But how can we be sure?

Is it fair that some people sit and watch destruction?
Their death is caused by illness, famine and poverty.

In this life we fight for what we want,
Some people watch it dissolve.
In our lifetime we can't escape the truth,
Something bad is always waiting.

Is it fair that people have gold and riches?
All they seem to think about is me, myself and I.

We all have our dreams, together we can succeed,
But we need everyone's ambitions to get what we need.

Georgia James (13)
Camden School for Girls

Fighting With Light

There was a man who tried despite
The war, the fighting, blood and might,
To make the world a better place
With only peacefulness and grace.

He was loved by all his people,
Deeply hated by all things evil,
For he could overcome their might,
By doing what he knew was right.

His name was Gandhi and he would fight
Not with violence, but with light.

Natasha Feinstein (13)
Camden School for Girls

Parts

Us sitting here eating breakfast, lunch and dinner
Every day,
But they have to get water,
This is a mile away.
Our generation is so ungrateful for what we have got,
But they sit in the darkness with things that rot,
And we have education,
No need to pay,
But they have to work, day by day.
3 course meals every day,
But they're there with no room to play.
The point I'm trying to prove is harsh, I know,
But people might disagree with me though,
It is true that we are sometimes spoilt and rude,
They don't give their mums attitude!
What I'm trying to say is,
Reduce our stuff,
Because they don't have enough.

Michiko Vidal-Newman
Camden School for Girls

Ostrich

I dream of breaking free
Of breaking free from the prison of my body
The body that can't fly
My scaly legs can only walk
My beak will never snatch fish from the foamy seas
My eyes will never sight the snowy-peaked mountains
And my breath will never taste the cool moisture of the

gentle clouds.

My dream is further than I can reach
My dream is to break free and fly.

Polly Evans
Camden School for Girls

17

I Have A Dream

I have a dream to be the only one,
The only one,
Who can change the world.
To change the world to be a friendly place,
To not be resistant to other people.

But I'm only 11,
What can I do?
I can't do that much you know!
The world is big,
I just can't change it
Just like that you know!

Maybe if I'm older,
And mature enough.
But that might be me,
To be that person,
You never know what you could be!
It could be you too!

Ishrat Chowdhury
Camden School for Girls

Untitled

In my perfect world the songbird sings, the cool water laps
At the cushioning sand and the sun sparkles down
Through the sapphire sky. There's a tree,
In a white-walled garden with a million. The golden gate is closed.
The fruit through the smooth golden bars looks luscious,
Peaches plump, oranges bending the branches of the tall tree,
Trying to touch the ground.
I reach out, trying to grab the most heavenly of the fruits.
But as soon as I touch the smooth surface,
The world spins away and the Utopia is gone.

Stella Scobie (12)
Camden School for Girls

I Have A Dream

I have a dream that the animals could speak
That they could express their feelings and emotions
That they could stick up for what they believe in

I have a dream that all the animal cruelty could stop
All the slaving and beating could stop
All the torture and unfairness could stop

I have a dream that animals will have rights
The right to live undisturbed by our constant quest
Our constant quest to have more land, more things, more meat

I have a dream that we will value all animals
Not just for what they do for us
But for the beauty and joy they give us

My dream is a dream of fairness for animals
Have you had this dream too?

Rachel Cullen (12)
Camden School for Girls

I Have A Dream

My heart is pumping
My palms are sweating
The trigger is pulled
And the impulse kicks in
My vision is blurred
And I can barely feel my feet
The end seems so far from here
The noises all come to a halt
I so badly want to stop
But I just have to go on
When I cross the line there is a tremendous cheer
Then finally I'm done.

I've won!

Farah Charles
Camden School for Girls

I Have A Dream

Imagine a world where teachers weren't such bores,
Where children never had to do their chores,
Where there was no fighting, violence, guns or wars,
I have a dream.

Imagine a world where everyone had food and water,
Where everyone was able to have a son or daughter,
Where playtime was long and lessons shorter,
I have a dream.

Imagine a world where we could fly,
Where there was no such thing as telling a lie,
Where you would never ever have to die,
I have a dream.

Susannah Fairbank Angus (12)
Camden School for Girls

I Have A Dream

The time has finally come which I've prepared for ages.
The whirling butterflies in my belly rages,
The large crowds are all shouting and screaming,
I can see with excitement, their eyes are gleaming,

Should I give up now before it's too late?
What if winning isn't my fate?
A voice inside my head tells me to persevere,
I repeat it again and again to help my fear.

My heart starts thumping extremely loud,
I hope I make my country proud.
The impatience which I cannot hold,
To wonder if I'll take home the gold.

Emma Khan
Camden School for Girls

I Have A Dream

I have a dream that I can be free
And travel the world,
I have a dream to help disabled people
Swim with dolphins,
I have a dream to make people glad and proud
Of me in what I do,
I have a dream to make people see what I can do
If I really try,
I have a dream that there will be no shooting
And killing in the world,
I have a dream that there will be peace
In the world.

Connie McGuire (13)
Camden School for Girls

Gates Of The World

(Inspired by Miranda Gates)

Not a spiralled rusty obstacle but a person
Open arms encouraging
Unity and understanding
Where work is amongst a different race to your own.
Life at a level you never had intended
The strife of Man forever unperceived
Is that of gates to the future,
Unity through open gates
In the community of the world.

Emily Doyland (13)
Camden School for Girls

Old Dog Of War

In the scarred wastelands of what used to be a country
He howls,
With the blood of others on his hands
He howls,
Being told he is bringing justice and sanctity
He howls,
Being told he is a true patriot
He howls,
With memories that are good and bad
He howls,
Unaware he is being used
He howls,
Fighting in a pointless struggle
He howls,
With justice in his mind but unknown evil in his cause
He howls,
Howling for justice, howling for peace
And howling for an end to war
This old Dog of War isn't being heard,
Instead he is being used in a pointless massacre
Blind to the injustice,
So for once, let us hear his howls, this is my dream.

Emad Baitghanem Hezani (14)
Capital City Academy

I Have A Dream

'I have a dream'
Spoken by a man with one thing in mind,
For everyone to be equal,
Everyone on top and no one left behind.

I once had a dream,
It was a place where there was no war,
Everyone was happy,
And everyone obeyed the law.

There was no pollution,
Just a clean world
Where people lived cheerfully
Where everyone's inner happiness unfurled.

Children playing outside without fear of danger,
Mums and dads never needing to have a worry,
Kids played as long as they wanted,
But for sweets and food, they came back in a hurry.

This is my dream
For you to see
Maybe one day
This is what the world would be.

Gopal Ladva
Capital City Academy

I Have A Dream

America, the world it has changed
Everyone is equal in every way,
The dream has come true
But not completely,
There is still a bit of racism
In different parts of the world
Towards different people,
But one day the dream will be complete.

Liam Scott-McGhee
Capital City Academy

I Have A Dream

I have a dream that one day
There will be no killing.

I have a dream that one day
People can do what they're willing.

So stop the rude texting,
Go home and start resting.

People will be more safe
Walking on the streets with more faith.

Those gangs need to stop
So they don't flop.

Leave the knives and the guns
And find another way to make your funds.

So from now on . . .

I want to be able to walk safe on the streets,
Without hearing gunshots or police cars
Because someone died,
Or there's a fight between gangs.

Just stop the *crime!*

Jessica Dos Santos
Capital City Academy

24

I Have A Dream

I have a dream, that one day
Unfortunate people with no food or water
Would have something to eat and drink.
I have a dream, that one day teenage crimes would stop,
Full stop!
And that people would feel safe and free
Walking on the streets without carrying weapons for protection.
I have a dream, that one day cigarettes and harmful drugs
Would be banned,
And that the world would become smoke and drugs free.
I have a dream, that one day
People would stop littering and start recycling.
I have a dream, that one day homeless people and vagrants
Would have some place cosy to live.
I have a dream, that one day abused pets and animals
Would be treated with care.
I have a dream, that one day abandoned and neglected children
Would be loved and take care of.
But this, ladies and gentlemen, is just a dream,
Why don't you help make this dream come into reality
So that everybody would be happy and treated equally?

Hebaq Hassan
Capital City Academy

I Have A Dream That's All About Rats

I have a dream,
That rats will be loved everywhere
And that they will not be discriminated against
Because of the sewers and the plague.

I have a dream,
That scientists will no longer
Test on them for health and beauty products,
Poke them with needles and torture them until death.

I have a dream,
That everyone will have pet rats,
Love and care for them,
And realise they are clean and not dirty.

I have a dream
That everyone will want one,
That instead of a dog being a man's best friend
A rat will be man's best friend.

I have a dream,
That all these dreams will come true,
And rats will rule the world.

Laura Batchelor (14)
Capital City Academy

I Have A Dream

I have a dream,
That I can breathe fresh air
That's not polluted by cars and planes.
I have a dream,
That Barack Obama will do good
For the nation of America.
I have a dream,
That my teenagers can go
Outside and not be afraid of
Getting shot.
I have a dream,
That my voice and others will be heard.
I have a dream,
To look into the night sky and
Not see flashing lights.
I have a dream
That the economic slump will end.
I have a dream,
That tonight I will sleep peacefully
In my bed.

Alice Dagnino (14)
Capital City Academy

David Beckham

He's the fastest man
On the pitch, gifted
Like no one else, it's
David Beckham.

Legs that can run
Forever. Special like
A cheetah, he never
Puts less than 100% into every
Game.

Dedicated to his team
So you won't see him
Slacking, every day
Training, even though it's
Raining.

Swift as a snake
Cunning as a lion
He's the number one
David Beckham.

Joshua
Capital City Academy

My Inspiration Poem

My parents are my heroes
And they are as kind as sunlight
My parents are the best you can ever have
Because they never fight.

My parents are my heroes
They always stand by me
When I need help they are there
They make me feel free.

My parents are my heroes
They helped me get a roof
Over my head no matter what
They always tell the truth.

My parents are my heroes
They always bring happiness to me,
My parents are my heroes
And I'm sure you'll all agree.

Kyra Anderson
Capital City Academy

Imagine

Imagine
A place with no guns and no violence
Imagine
A sea where you can see down to the bottom
Imagine
A world with no rules
Imagine
Eating things you like and getting fitter
Imagine
Having everything you ever wanted
Imagine, imagine, imagine,
Let your mind wander!

Alfie Ashton (12)
City of London Academy

Sunny Day

On one sunny day
Barack Obama became American president
On one sunny day
Someone won an Oscar in Hollywood
On one sunny day
Will Smith stunned the world with his new film
On one sunny day
Chris Hoy won the world Olympic bike riding in Beijing
On one sunny day
Bugatti made the brilliant Veyron
On one sunny day
I went to a beautiful place
On a sunny bright day
My mum inspired me to be good at what I do
And then it happened, I became a star.

Jack Brown (12)
City of London Academy

My Favourite Author: Jacqueline Wilson

I wish I could write as well as her
And quickly get it all done
Sell all my copies of a book
Turning into a hit in London.

The ideas would just pour out of me
Like a storybook in my head
I'd start to write pages and pages
Following in the footsteps she led.

She has the best selling books
She is my inspiration
She is who I want to meet one day
She is Jacqueline Wilson!

Natasha Milton-Hunter (13)
City of London Academy

Change

If I could change anything
I would change how the guns and knives are on the street
Another parent crying because of the loss of a loved one
Roses are red
Violets are blue
Put guns and knives down
Cause the next victim
Might
Be
You.

Sharvina Watson (13)
City of London Academy

You Can Do It

If you want to do it, you can do it
Always put your mind to it
Never give up
Never look down
Always have a smile on your face
And see yourself in a better place.

Patrice Salmon (13)
City of London Academy

I Have A Dream

I have a dream that people will not pollute the Earth.
I have a dream that people will not do drugs
Or anything that will hurt their bodies.
I have a dream that people will not hurt or kill other people
Because they feel like it, or just for fun.
I have a dream that you will dream these same things,
Just like I do.
So don't be afraid to dream.

I have a dream that people would stop hating each other.
I have a dream that world hunger would end.
I have a dream that there is world peace.
I have a dream that money won't take over the world.
I have a dream that pollution will end.
I have a dream that sickness will end.
I have a dream that people will be equal.
I have a dream that people will respect me for who I am.
I have a dream that everybody would have this dream.

Urussa Khan (11)
Connaught School for Girls

Inspiration

I nspire someone.
N ever think it's wrong.
S ee what is right.
P ick a person you know.
I ntelligent brains can work.
R elate it to you.
A mbitions can grow.
T alent all day.
I t could be you one day.
O ne day it will.
N othing can be a dream.

Adina Suleman (12)
Connaught School for Girls

I Have A Dream

Devastation hitting like an earthquake
Destroying buildings and the lives they take.
I have a dream.

Blood and horror on every person's face
On July 7th the country was a disgrace.
I have a dream.

I have a dream to stop terrorism
Maybe it will become true.
I have a dream to stop terrorism
And I have a point to prove.

Hell and fury had a message to send
Maybe the chaos will come to an end.
I have a dream.

Does the world have to be this way?
Why don't we make peace today?
I have a dream.

I have a dream to stop terrorism
Why don't we do it now?
I have a dream to stop terrorism
But the question is, how?

If this carries on more people will die
If this carries on children will cry.
I have a dream.

If this stops this world will be fine
If this stops the world will shine.
I have a dream.

I have a dream to stop terrorism
As crazy as it may seem.
I have a dream to stop terrorism
What is your dream?

Abdi Mahamud (11)
Drayton Manor High School

I Have A Dream

Boom! Crash!
The world stands still.
Bang! Yell!
Terrorists who like to kill.

Shriek! Cry!
Babies dying of hunger.
Croak! Whimper!
People dying younger and younger.

I have a dream,
Where there is no war.
I have a dream,
Where hunger is no more.

I have a dream,
Where we breathe clean air.
I have a dream,
Where people will care.

I have a dream,
It's more of a fantasy.
I have a dream,
It helps me through reality.

Hannah Jones-Bedward (13)
Drayton Manor High School

I Have A Dream

Stop.
Look around you.
What do you see?
I see destruction, blood and terror,
It seems to go on forever and ever.

Stop.
Look around you.
What do you want?
A Utopia filled with love and peace,
All wars *have* to cease.

Stop.
Look around you.
What do you see?
I see changes
About to happen.

Rebecca Ryan (11)
Drayton Manor High School

The Night I Had A Dream

One night I had a dream
However far from reality it may seem
People were all equal, racism didn't exist
No such thing as fighting, no need for the fist
Illnesses and diseases went away
Their innocent victims came back to live another day
The trees were growing big and strong
The streets were welcoming, nothing was wrong
Orphans with their parents were as happy as can be
Their innocent prisoners were all set free
Then I woke up to see my dream was far from reality
I want my dream to be reality now
The only question is, how?

Georgina Ledwith (13)
Drayton Manor High School

I Have A Dream

An ideal world would be one where
Everything is just and fair

No wars, no fighting, no bloodshed
No orphans with their parents dead

No one starving, no one poor
A fragile Earth that is cared for

'Let's have that world!' I want to scream
Well, why not? I have a dream.

Katharine Swindells (12)
Drayton Manor High School

Dreams

I had a dream
A dream I influenced the world
The good, the bad, everyone.

Everyone has a dream
Maybe a big one like owning a massive company
Or a small one like owning a shop
But every dream can come true
It pops out of the blue
Leading you to big clues.

A special wish is a dream come true
Never give up your dream
Not for anyone
If you think you can complete your dream
Complete it
Slowly, slowly, bit by bit.

No dream is a bad dream
Every dream leads to success
Every dream is one of the best.

Hashim Aziz (12)
Hampstead School

Stop The War

I dream for happiness
I dream for peace,
I dream that one day
I'll see my niece.

But the war is here,
And I'm scared out of my mind,
I want to run away,
Leave this hell behind.

I'm cold, I'm wet,
I'm soaking to the core,
I see deaths all around me,
I can't take it anymore.

They said there was help,
They said it was here,
I pray that the end
Of the war is near.

There's a bullet in my arm,
My life crumbling in me,
My wife's given birth
To a son I'll never see.

I leave you now,
I see the light is near,
This is the end of me
I cry my last tear.

Alex Cook (14)
Hampstead School

Life

Stop!
Please make it stop!
This way . . .
Does it always have to be this way?
I want to make it better
But how?
How does one 13-year-old girl from Cricklewood
Change the world?
At least I want to make it better,
But - how - do I change it?
Why - does it always have to be like this?
Where - is my place, if not like this?
When - will it stop?
What - can we do?
Who - am I to try?

But I will . . . I'll make this world a better place,
Even if it kills me.
I just want to make this living hell
That is their lives,
Better - even just for a week -

Better!

Jo Gowers (13)
Hampstead School

Jade Goody

'Mums don't die'
But sometimes they cry,
But maybe sometimes they lie
To save their children's life . . .

Most believe in Heaven
Most believe in Hell
Some believe in none.

But we stick together
For number one.

We care for our family,
We care for our souls
And now we say goodnight,
Cause your time has come
To see your family before you're gone . . .

When I'm a mum I am gonna be
To the best of my ability.

The end.

Samantha Mulhall (12)
Hampstead School

A Dream

A dream
Is a wishful thought,
A dream
Can come true,
A dream
Either little, such as a first kiss,
A dream
Grand, such as raising kids,
A dream
Will come true if you believe,
A dream
Is a fairytale come true,
A dream
Can last forever in your heart,
A dream
Is a wishful thought,
A dream
Will come true.

Zena Najdawi (12)
Hampstead School

I Have A Dream

I have a dream,
It's not horrid or mean,
I wanna be the light in the crowd,
I wanna be heard, I wanna be loud,
I wanna speak words that can change the world,
See my dreams unfold,
I wanna inspire others,
All the sisters and the brothers,
Imagine the pen is mightier than the sword,
Imagine it's not just the rich with the hoard,
I wanna be the one hand with a pen,
I wanna help the poor women and the men,
I have a dream
To change the world.

Simi Begum (12)
Hampstead School

I Have A Dream

A dream
That will one day come true,
A dream
I will be proud to tell the world,
A dream
To inspire other people,
A dream
I will let no one break,
A dream
That will change my life,
A dream
I will never forget,
A dream
To change the world.

Ranjila Azizi (12)
Hampstead School

41

Dream Poem

I magine millions of people's lives changed by one voice.

H earing the crowd chant my name as I change the world.
A rriving to see a better future for our generation.
V illages and towns surrounded by freedom.
E rupting crowds, living their dream.

A single dream, inspiring millions.

D reams that will live on forever.
R emembering how one voice is all you need.
E ntering fields of happiness and joy.
A new dawn on a peaceful Earth.
M ake your dreams come true, you can change the world.

Farid Habashi (12)
Hampstead School

I Have A Dream

I have a dream,
A perfect rose,
This is where
My future grows.

Some wish to help
The poor and blind,
Just to let their
Dreams unwind.

When I am older,
To be a vet,
Is exactly where
My dreams are set.

For the old and
For the young,
Their dreams
Have only just begun.

Loren Hunt (12)
Heathcote School

I Have A Dream

I have a dream,
That everyone will have a home,
A place that they can call their own,
Four walls and a roof above their heads,
A chair, a table and a bed.

I have a dream,
That no one will live on the streets,
Imagine losing everything that makes your life complete,
We all take things for granted sometimes, clothes, furniture, beds,
Some people have none of these,
Not even a roof above their heads.

I have a dream,
That no one will have to beg for money,
Some people don't take it seriously but this really isn't funny,
For some people this is the only way to get enough money for the week,
You wouldn't find it funny if it was your family on the streets.

I have a dream,
That young children won't have to grow up without a home,
Getting teased at school
Because they don't have a games console, money or phone.
For all these kids life can get too hard to handle, too tough,
But these are all realities for kids who are sleeping rough.

I have a dream,
Homelessness will be a thing of the past,
Something deep in history, let's make these sad cases the last.

Jodie Simmons (13)
Heathcote School

I Have A Dream

The future is bright
And all is light,
For people old and young
Can all have fun.

In the spring,
The joy it brings
To see a smiling face
Among the human race.

But sad times,
Without any rhymes,
When a child dies
Because of flies.

Just a little
Sum of money
Could help them sleep
Without a peep.

When I'm older,
I'll go with a folder
To help them out,
There's no reason to doubt.

I have a *dream*,
Like a shimmering stream,
Dreams can come true
For me and you.

Hannah Tyzack (12)
Heathcote School

My Future Dream

I have a dream that will surely reign,
Peace around in the sun and rain;
Living free of poverty,
Just live in harmony;
Although it's not how it'll seem,
I will surely have a dream.

I have a dream that's right for me,
I will have the world to see;
Maybe a celebrity,
Fame and fortune it will be;
Something made for all to redeem,
I will surely have a dream.

I have a dream to entertain,
Everybody free from pain;
Cure is found from all disease,
Let it happen, please oh please!
We will all work as a team,
I will surely have a dream.

I have a dream to know it all,
Know what has come to a fall;
Tell the future to everyone,
Oh, it will be so much fun!
Mysteries will be a beam,
I will surely have a dream.

Kaesi Opara (12)
Heathcote School

Drinking And Driving

I have a dream going out on a Saturday night,
Meeting up with my friends to party all night,
Sitting and chatting,
Smoking and drinking.

It's more fun just standing and dancing,
Lots of laughs and giggles too.
There's no more fun in throwing up over my shoes.

Walking and talking,
Looking around,
I think it's boring just sitting around.

What a fun night it would have been
If only I didn't drink all night and wasn't seen.
I didn't see the little dog crossing the road,
Even though I thought that I would have been told.

Turning around talking to my friends,
I should have kept my eyes on the road ahead.
With a scratch and thud
The poor dog is now dead.

What a stupid fool I was,
I should have taken the last bus instead,
No more drinking and driving for me,
The little dog would still be alive and at
Home with me.

The police were called
And said that I had to go to court,
If I didn't drink and drive
I wouldn't have been caught.

Now looking at a fine,
And banned from driving.
Life would be more interesting without
Drinking and driving.

I wish I had listened to my mum
Instead of the foolish girl I'd become.

Now I am at home alone with
No one to blame but me.
Now that my story has been told,
Please don't end up like me.

Stephanie Sloughly (14)
Heathcote School

War

War means death . . .
War means destruction . . .
War means fire . . .
War means bombing . . .
War means sorrow . . .
War means turmoil . . .
War means tears . . .
War means guns . . .
War means blood . . .
War means confusion . . .
War means explosions . . .
War means mutilation . . .
War means sickness . . .
War means killing . . .
War means occupation . . .
War means loss . . .
And lots more . . .

But after one side
Or the other side
Has finally had enough
And lays down their arms
To surrender and give up . . .

War means peace . . . !

John Kiely (13)
Heathcote School

I Have A Dream

I have a dream,
I dream that all children can feel safety and happiness.
On the outside they look like they're fine,
Like they're holding it all together.

But on the inside they're screaming.
They're trying to scream loud enough
For you to hear them but you can't.
No sound escapes.

They wish you could read their minds
Because they are scared to speak.
They wish they had strength and courage
To tell you how they feel.
Sometimes they feel as if nothing matters,
Their future, is it worth it?
That's why I dream to make it worth it.
Their present, all it is, is surviving one day to the next,
Just surviving.

I think they deserve a break,
Relief and a feeling of safety.

All children do, it's not fair until it is,
My dream will never end.

Shanel Nejat (12)
Heathcote School

I Have A Dream

I have a dream
That prisons have no cause,
That nobody breaks laws,
That there is no such thing as wars,
That I can open closed doors.

I have a dream
That we live in an easier time,
That the birds sing and chime,
That the world is free of crime,
That we all live in our prime.

I have a dream
That slaves in Africa are free,
That the blind are able to see,
That all animals were left be,
That everybody has a house key.

I have a dream
That I will make a difference,
That I will be remembered,
That I will make history,
That I will never be forgotten.

This is my dream.

Josiah Matheson (12)
Heathcote School

Cancer-Free World!

I have a dream
That cancer will be cured,
No one will die,
All be alive, happy and
Pure.
All women will live a
Healthy life,
And not die when they're
Meant to be a wife.
Men will be joyful,
Children will be merry,
Their children off to
School they will ferry.

The world will be cancer-free
No more injections in
Your knee.
No more unhappy families
No more crying with
Pain,
Live your life, there's a
Lot to gain.

Jamie Di-Valentine (13)
Heathcote School

I Have A Dream

Each and every one of us
Was born to make a *difference*.
We were born to make a *change*.
It is our job to choose a path,
A path to the future, you decide which one.
When the path seems to end
And you can't see the light,
Keep following and chasing your dream,
Put up a fight.
One day when you catch that dream,
Never let go and hold it tight.
Have love for each other,
Have love for your dream.
Don't let anyone get in the way
Of what you *want*,
Push through the boundaries,
They are the devils that walk among *us*.
Live your own dream,
Don't prevent others from living theirs.
Our life is our dream,
We are living our dream.

Jonathan Hoey (13)
Heathcote School

I Have A Dream

I have a dream that children will not fear
Or have constant reminders of their peers.
I have a dream where name calling will lead to praise,
When young people's thoughts will be clear but not in a maze.

I have a dream where children will not be judged
Or be afraid of walking down the street and being mugged.
I have a dream where children will be as brave as a knight
So they won't cry themselves to sleep at night.

I have a dream that children could walk down the street
And would not be hurt
And they would always stay alert.
I have a dream that children could let their hair down
And not be afraid of the other crowd.

I have a dream that children will not be afraid
By the remarks that were made.
I have a dream children will stand up for what's right
And then they will see the light
To where their dreams come true.

I have a dream . . . !

Channon Bramwell (12)
Heathcote School

I Have A Dream

I won't let it get to me,
I will think only optimistic thoughts.
I will go back to school,
I will go to my first party,
I will pursue my dreams.
I will achieve my every goal in life,
Well - at least I will try.

I will do everything kids my age do,
I will spend more time with my family.
I will go round my friend's house and order pizza,
We will watch films and stay up late.
I will try and do everything to the best of my ability.

I will return the support my friends and family have given me.

I will one day find my true love and get married . . .
Maybe!
Children . . . who knows?
But one thing I do know,
I *will* survive.

Rhianna Lee (13)
Heathcote School

I Have A Dream

I have a dream, such a dream
Of no guns or knives
But beautiful flowers that smell so nice,
Let loose the white doves of peace.

No wars, no fights,
But our civil rights.
Crimes not allowed
So we should speak out loud,
Speak for our human race,
Live long and be proud.

Jade-Marie Eaton (12)
Heathcote School

Life On The Streets

I hope one day I will eat the banana
Not the skin,
I hope one day I will be looking in the cupboards
Instead of a bin.
I have a dream one day I will live in a house
Not a cardboard box,
And not be on the hunt, pouncing around like a fox.
I have a dream one day I will work
Instead of scavenging for money,
I wish to have a family
Instead of being so lonely.
I have a dream one day I will rest my head on a nice soft pillow
Instead of the hard pavement,
And I will eat a well-cooked fish
Not snails for Lent.
I wish to have a family,
Not a pet snail,
And I can go to the toilet
Instead of going to the rail.

Ismael Gonzalez-Patel (12)
Heathcote School

I Have A Dream

This poem is for every man or woman who made it.

Some people think they need to drink to make them happy,
But it makes them snappy.

Saddened eyes and weakened smiles,
Depressed all day and drunk all night.

But when they get help they see the light,
They figure out what's wrong and what's right.

Every day is clearer and brighter,
When you stop drinking and start thinking.

Romy Deighton (13)
Heathcote School

Nightmare Dream

I have a dream,
Not as big as world peace,
But something big to me,
And my dream is that
Communities stand together in abundance,
Like wine groves in northern Italy.

The world's dream is bigger than me,
Bigger than all of us, you could say,
But just remember your dream
And all the people around you,
Because the world is a community,
And being unique makes that community.

Fights and wars, segregation and violence
Is a nightmare in this world,
Being equal is close to corruption,
Remembering yesterday is forgetting tomorrow,
Freedom covers a book but does not fill it
In this nightmare world.

Joseph Loftus (13)
Heathcote School

I Have A Dream

I look forward to the day
When I can walk down the street
And watch everyone mix.
Black, white, rich or poor,
We are all but one.
I look forward to the day
When I walk past a mixed couple hand in hand
And I'm gonna feel proud that I stand out in the crowd,
It's not the colour of your skin,
It's what's within.

Natalie Robinson (13)
Heathcote School

I Have A Dream

Discrimination is a pain,
There is nothing to gain
Apart from making people feel ashamed
For being the colour that they are,
But we must forget about the past
And make sure the future comes fast
And look for the good times that may pass.

I have a dream
Where children will not be judged
By the colour of their skin,
And they will not feel
Like they are living in a bin.
I have a dream
That children could walk down their street,
Be proud of the way they looked
And will follow the rules by the book.

I have a dream
That this world will be full of peace.

Leon Burrows (12)
Heathcote School

I Have A Dream

I have a dream people will stop knife crime,
Only to have someone reduce their living time.
I hope people will understand if you do the crime
You have to pay the time.
Let's stop this crime so no one has to pay the time,
Let's make the most of this time and remember this line.
Don't make people extinct
Or then the human race will sink.

The end.

Meet Patel (13)
Heathcote School

I Have A Dream

I can't wait for the day when I get to go home,
I'm going to see my family
And eat a fresh hot meal from the stove,
I am going to sleep in a nice bed that belongs to me,
Instead of crouching on the floor
Wondering what my life could be.
I can't wait for the day
When I don't have to watch my friends die,
I'll have more friends, more than the bees in a hive.

But this is my job; I have to hold a gun,
I know for some it's not so much fun,
But war is necessary to give countries peace,
To give innocent people back their dignity
So they can live without fear,
For that reason, I have to be here
And fight this war,
So countries can thrive and have their own laws.

I have a dream.

Jamaal Otto (13)
Heathcote School

I Have A Dream

Imagine the headlines tomorrow
Stating that all illness has been wiped out,
There will be no funeral, no scream and shout,
Because mums and dads want to see their children grow.
There will be no more pain and no more freak shows.

Imagine no hospital queues or doctors poking you about,
Instead you lead your life eating, shopping or going out,
Because children want to grow up to be a plumber, decorator or nurse.
There will be enough money to get rid of the deadly curse.

Imagine the father walking his daughter down the aisle.
There will be happiness and no more tears
Because the parents want to see their grandchildren play.
Every innocent child deserves a second try without fears.

Imagine we could start tomorrow,
Where the world would be a place without sorrow,
I have a dream to get rid of all illnesses,
A dream filled with joy where every child could be healed.

Lisa Vu (12)
Heathcote School

I Have A Dream

I have a dream
That bullying will stop
And everyone will be fair
And people will be friendly pairs
If I see bullying it breaks my heart
And it stabs me like a dart.

If you see bullying it's like you getting a punch
You must stop pulling
And run away from the bunch.

Here I am at school feeling cool
And not a person that is feeling drool
I am feeling great that
I have fantastic mates.

When I get home
I am not on my own
I am with my loving mum
And I don't feel glum.

Ashley Greaves (12)
Heathcote School

I Have A Dream

I have a dream that the world
Will not be polluted.
CO_2 makes things overheated.
Global warming is making animals extinct,
Stop polluting so the Arctic will not sink.
Stop cutting down the trees or there won't be any bees
To help with pollination because we'll
Be extinct as a nation.

I have a dream that the sea will be pale blue
And the sky will be too.
Go green to recycle and save yourself.
Go as a community to stop car fuels,
To keep up your health and will
Stop your children getting the flu.
I have a dream that hopefully will come true.

I have a dream!

Daniel Gowan (13)
Heathcote School

I Have A Dream

I have a dream,
For torture to end,
That the world was full of peace,
And everyone to be friends.

I have a dream,
That cruelty was no more,
The Earth must live,
There must be no war.

If you have a dream,
That you want to come true,
Make it happen,
Do what you want to do.

Sophie White (12)
Heathcote School

60

I Have A Dream

Beating down on my bed
The cold wind and rain is taking over my head,
No roof, no warmth,
I had it all but it went away,
I look forward to the day.

I have a dream,
It will be all there,
My family, my friends,
Now they don't care,
They said I dug my own grave,
I guess I have to be brave.

Walking round in this mad world,
I'm alone in this cold
But I will find a nice home to grow old,
It will have a cooker, a heater and a bed,
But one day I am going to be warm not dead.

Oliver Carroll (12)
Heathcote School

Knife Crime . . .

This poem is for every survivor that made it,
Every guy who was insulted and hit.
My message is that we're going to drop the knife,
We're going to save another life.

For every knife that plunged through an innocent heart
We're going to turn a new leaf and make a new start,
Because we're going to drop the knife,
We're going to save another life.

For every argument that caused a fight,
We're going to put our mistakes right,
We're going to put down the knife,
And we're going to save another life!

Nabila Kunwar (13)
Heathcote School

Child Abuse

One more kick, one more punch,
Never getting any more munch,
I get one other bruise,
Dad buys even more booze.

No more love and care,
All the cupboards are so bare,
It's like I don't exist
Apart from when he throws a fist.

I have a dream
This will come to an end.
I have a dream
My life will mend.
I have a dream
I will not be in pain
I have a dream
There's more to life, to gain.

Sorcha Campbell (13)
Heathcote School

I Have A Dream

I dream of the day when I step into my house,
And don't have to sit as quietly as a mouse.
Mum and Dad argue, they never stop,
I wish I could leave or call the cops.
I want no shouting, screaming, fussing or fighting,
It's like a thunderstorm in my house, thunder and lightning.

Now they are apart it's torn my heart,
But I get two birthdays and two Christmases,
They spoil me rotten,
All that arguing I've completely forgotten.

I have a dream to grow up with a smile on my face,
Now my parents are sorted, I feel part of the human race.

Becki Hardcastle (13)
Heathcote School

Stop Smoking

Lung cancer and heart disease,
Stop smoking, please stop, please,
It's addictive, dangerous and unhealthy,
Not to mention, it decreases your chance of being wealthy.
I sit and watch people puffing away,
And wonder whether you will live another day,
Inhaling chemicals, tobacco and don't forget tar,
Don't you realise you're smoking stuff in your car?

But if you stop and throw the fags away,
There will be a chance you could live another day,
You will feel a lot happier, pleasant and proud,
Need to leave the other addicts, find a new crowd.
After a while you will wonder why you didn't stop sooner,
You won't grow up looking like an old crooner,
So stop, throw those cigarettes away,
Stop today and live another way!

Nicole Clark (13)
Heathcote School

The Knives Kill

No more knives in my life
I want my family to feel safe,
Kids on the street left to weep.
These knives kill, your body ends up still,
It's time to get real or you could
Be the next one killed.
Kids be aware
And take care.
The knife crime is about who is the better gang,
If you get drawn in you'll end up with the bang.
I have a dream to get out there and help these kids,
Show them the right path.
I have a dream and I'm gonna take the cream.

Scott Blenheim-Aning (12)
Heathcote School

I Have A Dream

I have a dream that parents will finally take care,
Because their children are running wild everywhere.
We need them to go to clubs, instead of going into the pubs
Because if they do the crime,
They have to serve the time.
So instead of trouble and strife,
Tell them to get a life,
Because without your help and without your support,
They will end up in court.
So just think, if you let it carry on you'll visit them in prison,
And by then it will be too late to listen.
So I hope this poem makes you realise
That anti-social behaviour is a really big size,
So do the world a favour,
And stop this bad behaviour.

I have a dream.

Matthew Whyman (13)
Heathcote School

Knives!

Is it hard to say no to knives?
Or is it better to save a life?
Plenty of youths are dying every day,
It is us to blame for letting them stray?

I have a dream to make it a better place,
Where you don't get stabbed for being a different race.
We need to think of the positive
Instead of being scared
That someone will find out where you live.

This dream will come true if everyone together,
Not just me, but black, Asian, Turkish
And white too.

Astrit Loshaj (13)
Heathcote School

Put It Down

Put it down, just put the knife down,
Let it go, just let it go,
Laugh, smile and dream,
Think of what we could have been.
But seriously, put it down, just put the knife down,
Let it go, just let it go,
It glints in the moonlight,
You're starting to scare me.

Put it down, just put the knife down,
Let it go, just let it go,
Prison isn't right for you,
Heaven isn't ready for me,
We can still be friends,
Let me live my life,
Let yourself live yours,
So, seriously, just put the knife down.

Henry Wisbey-Broom (14)
Heathcote School

I Have A Dream

I have a dream,
That the world will be in peace,
That maybe,
You'll live to see your nephew and your niece.

I have a dream,
That cruelty to animals will stop,
So that you can see snakes sliding,
And see the bunnies hop!

I have a dream,
And I hope you'll help me
To help stop cruelty,
And have everything to see!

Hollie Harwood (11)
Heathcote School

I Have A Dream

I have a dream
And to me it gleams
It has paws
But is never a bore,
What is my dream?

It includes beagles and pugs
Taken by thugs,
And with my help they will never get hurt,
But they do roll around in the dirt.
What is my dream?

Well, have you had a guess?
They really can make a mess
So guess, guess, take a guess,
What is my dream?

Yes, I want to work for Dogs Trust.

Charlotte Gurfer (11)
Heathcote School

Knife Crime

No one wants their kids growing up in a mess
No one wants to get stabbed in the chest
No one wants pointed knives in their faces
No one wants to go out of the houses and have worried faces.

Kids get scared playing at the park
Kids get scared sitting in the dark
Kids get scared it might happen to them
Kids get scared it might hurt them.

Now it's time to change our life
Now it's time to put down the knife
Now it's time to end my rhyme
Now it's time to stop knife crime.

Jessica Ball (13)
Heathcote School

I Have A Dream

I have a dream
As big as can be
To make the streets a better place
For you and me.

I have a dream
As wide as can be
To help the ill
Make them feel better in time
So they are able to shine.

I have a dream
As huge as can be
To help the poor
So they can achieve more.

Phyllis Denkyi (13)
Heathcote School

I Have A Dream

I have a dream.

H onesty rules over dishonesty.
A buse dies down.
V ile people turn into pleasant beings.
E nd of all wars.

A vengers will be no more.

D isease will be eradicated.
R espect will be reciprocated.
E quality will be prerequisite material in all establishments.
A iding and abetting becomes an offence.
M oney wouldn't have to create a gap between rich and poor.

Gemma Dowsett (12)
Heathcote School

I Have A Dream!

H aving a roof over my head,
O ne that I own with my own bed.
M y dream is to live like others,
E at at the table,
L ive life to the fullest,
E veryone is able.
S omeday my life will be the best,
S earching through cupboards instead of bins,
N o more cold sleepless nights,
E verybody off the streets,
S top getting gnat bites,
S it in my own seats.

Gemma Phillips (12)
Heathcote School

Child Abuse

Late at night and I'm all alone
All I want to do is pick up the phone
Get out of this place and help myself
I'll be able to boost up my health.

I hear the door open and my heart starts to sink
I've got no time to think
He's coming up to me drunk, as he always does
Puts his hand on my mouth, and says, 'Shh, don't fuss.'

I finally had the courage to get some help
Now he's gone and I have no need to yelp,
At last I'm free, and happy!

Sophie Woodcock (14)
Heathcote School

Mummy's Girl

My mum is the best mum in the world,
She even calls me her favourite little girl,
She loves me very, very much,
She seems to have this special touch,
She gives me lots and lots of treats
That no other mum could beat.

I love my mum very much!

Mummy's girl is my name,
No other girl has the same,
Mummy always gives me money to spend
And I always buy the latest trends,
My mum is so kind and nice,
I don't even have to name a price.

I love my mum very much!

She always helps me when I fall
And answers as soon as I call,
My mum taught me how to brush my hair,
Tie my shoes and times and square,
She always treats me with love and care,
And always has enough to share,
She loves me and my little brother,
And to her it is no bother.

I love my mum very much!

Zoe Mannah (12)
La Retraite RC Girls' School

I Believe

I believe that one day there will be no war.
I believe that one day, no more famine.
I believe that with the help of everyone
And the help of anyone
This world can be a better place.

I believe that maybe today, maybe tomorrow,
There will be no more knife and gun crime.
I believe that *you* can make that happen.
I believe that there is no such thing as magic
But if you try hard enough you can make
What you do magic.

I believe that even if your voice
Is the tiniest in the room
It can still be heard even over the loudest.
I believe that your opinions are meant to be valued
So even if people don't want to listen then make them listen!

But do you know what I believe in the most?
I believe that everyone is equal,
No matter what school you go to, or what area you live in,
Everyone is equal.
It doesn't matter if you don't have the best education,
Or the best upbringing,
You are as important as anyone else.

Jade Nzekwe (12)
La Retraite RC Girls' School

My Dream

I have a dream . . .

I have a dream that one day we can
Overcome all the obstacles that we face in life,
I have a dream that one day we cannot be judged
For our wrongs in the past -
But for what we do now, and in the future,
I dream that one day there will be less killing,
So that we will not be afraid of leaving our homes,
I dream that one day we won't have to see
Innocent people being killed by the gang culture
That surrounds our society,
I dream that one day people
Would be able to live their lives freely,
I dream that one day everyone would be what they want to be,
So that this world can be a better place
For ourselves, our children and their children,
I dream for people to live their dreams,
This is what I dream for
I dream for this to be a reality.

Emma Ekpo (12)
La Retraite RC Girls' School

My Nan

My nan is a supernan
She cleans those pots and pans spick and span,
My nan is great
She's my best mate,
On the date
The 6th of March 2008
She took me to the Tate
And was a good candidate,
My nan is nice
She likes jollof rice.

Miclane Poleon-Mendez (12)
La Retraite RC Girls' School

The Future - A Bleak Place

The birds in the trees
The grass on the ground
Will no longer be there
When our grandchildren come around.

We are destroying the Earth
With our toxic pollution
Our greenhouse gases
And industrial revolution.

Look at what we're doing to our home!
We need to stop wasting our goods
Let's start to recycle because
The filth is destroying our neighbourhoods.

Think about it this way
If we don't help the future's pace
The future will be an extremely
Bleak place!

Andreia Nogueira (12)
La Retraite RC Girls' School

God's Flower Garden

The world is like a flower garden,
Each person having its own
Colour, crease, wrinkle or spot.
Despite our uniqueness we are all
Flowers in this world, our
Appearance may not be pleasing
To everyone, but take a look into
A mirror, look what you've got,
Love what you see, appreciate
What you see, then others will
Begin to appreciate you!

Destara Hird (11)
La Retraite RC Girls' School

Reduce, Reuse and Recycle

Do you wanna save the trees?
Well you'd better put down your keys,
And forget about the dailies
Even if it means daydreams,
Cos it'll help save the trees!

Do you wanna save the trees?
Cos you'll be saving fees
And reusing your files
To keep you going for miles
Whilst saving the trees!

Do you wanna save the trees?
Well you'd better get on your knees
And pick up all the paper
Even if it's a lot later,
And save the trees!

Chantelle Clottey (11)
La Retraite RC Girls' School

I Am The World And The World Is I

I am the world and the world is I,
I stand against racism and I fly so high,
I am neither black nor white, but orange, blue and red,
I am an array of colours like the butterfly that flutters.

I am the world and the world is I,
I am a combination of countries
That love to land each other punches,
Why can't we be together forever and ever?

I am the world and the world is I,
But soon I will be going,
As pollution will soon stop my rivers from flowing,
So take good care of me as I take care of you,
For I am the world and the world is I.

Morenike Agoro (11)
La Retraite RC Girls' School

God's World

We have been given an amazing opportunity
The opportunity to walk on God's Earth
To see all his amazing creations.

But we are taking his beautiful world for granted
We are clouding over the bright blue skies
We are poisoning his fresh water seas
We are cutting down his sweet smelling trees
We are putting God's world and God's creations in danger.

But how would you feel if you were God
See all this happen to your amazing world?
He made this world for people to love each other and share peace.
Not to cause hurt, war and hatred.

Just think for one minute, if you were God, what would you do?

Lilly-Ann Bell (11)
La Retraite RC Girls' School

Believe

Believe that you have the power
That can change you for life,
Imagine yourself as God's flower,
Try not to become the Devil's knife.

Believing makes you a better person,
Being deceived leads you downhill,
Seek for what you've always wanted,
After all the hard work, don't stand still.

Believing is what I've done for years,
You all know I'm not the only one,
Some people have tried, but overtaken by fear,
Me helping others in life is all I've ever done.

Niyat Joseph (12)
La Retraite RC Girls' School

I Am Me

I am me,
And I have a dream
To be who I want to be.

Live life to the full,
And always remember
You are you, and you are *beautiful!*

Rudeen Evans (12)
La Retraite RC Girls' School

I Have A Dream

I have a dream
To become important,
So that I can change the world
Into a better place.

I have a dream
To own a library
So that I can read a lot
Of beautiful stories.

I have a dream
To see in the future
So that I can predict
People's happiness.

I have a dream
To become famous
So that I walk on a red carpet
And smile at the cameras.

I have a dream
That people will choose their jobs
So that they can be free
And mostly happy.

I have the dream that all my dreams will come true!

Alexandra Zaoui (11)
Lycée Français Charles de Gaulle

My Dream For A Better World

I have a dream
Like many others
That gives me courage
Every day.

I dream of a place
Where a poppy will grow
Next to a tank,
And doves fly in the sky.

I dream of a place
Where there are no
Black, thick fumes
Rising in the air.

I dream of a place
Where butterflies
Fly freely in a city
Watched by eager children.

I dream of a place
Where a mother
On a hot continent
Doesn't need to see her son die.

I dream of a place
Where there are no children
Terrified in their beds,
Praying not to be beaten.

I dream of a place
Where every man
Can walk up to any other
And shake their hand without prejudice.

And all I wish
Is for my dream to come true.

Thomas Corbani (12)
Lycée Français Charles de Gaulle

I Have A Dream

I have a dream
To fly
I have a dream
To touch the sky
I have a dream
To jump from high
And survive!

I have a dream
To be the queen
To rule the world
Without being seen
To be the best
To beat the rest!

I have a dream
To save the planet
To be green and clean
And save the rabbits!

I have a dream
To grow a seed
That will be big and tall
And climbable
To find a house in the sky
And find the monster who lives up high!

I have a dream
To find a treasure
On a far away land
Underneath sand
I'll become rich and famous
And known as the girl
Who found the treasure!

Natascha Ouwerx-Wade (11)
Lycée Français Charles de Gaulle

World Of My Dreams

An ideal world only for me,
A unique place of fantasy,
Strange animals flying around,
No money, no dollar, no pound.
I'm the one they're dancing for,
With all this, I want no more!

I have a dream, a lone dream,
Just to be as happy as I seem,
A shining sun keeping me warm,
A farandole of colours, nothing will harm.
Nothing's better, that's for sure,
What mystery is this nature?

In this world there's all I need,
Nothing left I need to seed,
A shy moon, a cloudy night,
May the stars bring up so light.
I have a dream I can't deny,
In this world I want no lie.

Simple thoughts to imagine
The fairy world I'm living in,
Little creatures to entertain,
Nothing's hidden, there's no pain.
I'm seeing in the sky up high,
It's funny, I don't know why!

Full of colours is the rainbow,
Seeing this, I just say, 'Woah!'
I want to dance, I want to sing,
Things that really mean something.
This is a world I won't forget,
This is how I'd like the real one to get!

Victoire Ribert (13)
Lycée Français Charles de Gaulle

My Dream . . .

Last night I had a dream,
I was jumping high up in the sky,
I was touching the clouds,
I was almost flying,
Because in my dreams
Gravity has no hold
And time has no meaning.
But then a dark, looming shadow
Pushed me off my cloud,
And my landing point had disappeared,
My hair was standing up on end,
And my eyes were sealed shut,
I was falling down and down.
I felt my heart thumping harder and harder,
My stomach turning round and round,
I was scared.
My shoes came off,
One hit me in the face,
I felt a tear rolling down my cheek,
The darkness was taking over,
I was lost, like a little girl in a forest,
Except that I had no way out,
Nothing to hold onto.
I was tumbling down and down,
Out of existence,
Out of reality,
I was screaming and shouting,
I'm screaming and shouting,
But no one could hear,
So I continued falling, down this hole, that had no bottom,
Then, I woke up.

Julia Cox (13)
Lycée Français Charles de Gaulle

I Have A Dream

Some children are lucky,
They want everything.
But they should be grateful,
About what they have.

Some children spend the day
In the rubbish dump,
Searching for scraps,
For a bit of money.

Some children have a phone,
Others don't know what one is.
Some live in welcoming homes,
Many just live in a derelict shack.

Darwin would call that
Natural selection.
If only the wealthy kids
Would help the poor kids.

Some children have scary lives.
Some children have drunk parents,
Violent carers, disabled guardians.
They can't study and gain knowledge.

Lots of children do not have
The chance to learn at school.
To have a good job, a good life,
You need a good education.

Some children have serious illnesses,
They need our support and kindness.
I have a great life,
And I dream that everyone did too.

Fionn Royer-Gray (11)
Lycée Français Charles de Gaulle

Little Jonny Dee's Dream

Maths on Monday, music on Tuesday,
English on Wednesday, sports on Thursday,
French on Friday. Phew, it's Saturday!
I knew that school was coming to an end
But when precisely would this torture end?
I have a dream
When I came home I heard a plea:
'Come here Jonny, it's your mummy.
I've got your school report, let's look inside shall we?'
And at that off came my smile:
I knew I hadn't exactly been docile.
I have a dream
'What's this I see my little Dee?'
Came that same voice, devoid of glee
'Moany on Monday, terrible on Tuesday,
Whinging on Wednesday, not to mention Thursday,
Frightful on Friday. That's all there is to say!'
I have a dream
At that Mum's brainbox went kaput:
She started chasing me like some mad mutt!
'OK, OK, I'm sorry,' I shouted,
'Just give me a chance, I'll get it all sorted.'
But nothing could calm the old hag;
When she caught me, she shook me like a rag.

I've written this to show you all:
Be good at school or your mum will get cruel!

Louis Clement-Harris (11)
Lycée Français Charles de Gaulle

I Have A Dream

They all run away from me.
I want my freedom.
I want someone who loves me.

Jules Rognoni
Lycée Français Charles de Gaulle

I Have A Dream

I have a dream:
To live in books
Where myths are reality
And legends diamond hooks.

I have a dream:
To meet someone famous
Someone *everybody* knows.
We'd eat something scrumptious
And forget all our woes!

I have a dream:
To draw so well
That my work was
Too easy to sell.
During the day my store was a buzz,
I could not see,
What was all the fuss?

But my real dream
Would be to live in a world
Where everyone has money,
Where everyone is happy,
Where no one is hungry,
Where no wars exist
So when children rest their sleepy head
Have no worries before they go to bed.

Deborah Herzberg (11)
Lycée Français Charles de Gaulle

I Have A Dream

I have a dream that I need my friends,
Imagine that I've lost my magic,
My blue skies are too grey today.

I feel my passion has gone away,
I imagine that I'm losing myself,
I have a dream my soul has gone,
I am dreaming that I had a bad day today,
Because I lost all of my friends,
Forever and ever.
All of a sudden I'm having another dream,
It's summer, summertime is near,
I've been good but I can't wait,
It's been too long that I've been waiting.
I wish summer could come quickly,
I can hardly stand the wait,
Please summer, don't be late.
Please don't be late.

I am imagining in the dream that I've lost my friends forever,
I think they have gone forever.
Suddenly a hand is tendered to me,
He is my friend who is protecting me.
Now I'm sure he wouldn't, or they wouldn't,
Abandon me forever.

I wake up.

Byron Oputa (11)
Lycée Français Charles de Gaulle

I Have A Dream

I have a dream that one day this nation
Will rise up and . . . ban school education.

Why does every child have to go to school?
It's boring, dull and so not cool!

Adults say that for our future, we need an education,
But what's the point of doing maths calculations
If I've got a calculator? And why learn to spell
When my dictionary knows it very well?
Why do I have to learn how to play the flute?
I'd rather learn the trumpet and go *toot-toot-toot!*

I have a dream that one day this nation
Will . . . remove all teachers from the entire population!

Why can't I just play football all day?
Why can't grammar and arithmetic go away?
Geography and history, they bore me to my bones,
Why can't they just leave me alone?
School is so annoying, where I'd rather be
Is lying on the sofa watching good TV.

If it wasn't for my parents, for stupid Mum and Dad
I'd never go to school again, for that I'd be so glad.

I have a dream that children will one day
Live in a nation where . . . all they do is play!

Samuel Fitoussi (12)
Lycée Français Charles de Gaulle

I Have A Dream

School and dreams are completely different
For one thing you don't have to sit in a boring science lesson
Having a teacher watching you with a rather stern expression
I would prefer to be in the place of my dreams,
Sitting here, oh how boring it seems!

In your dreams you can have loads of fun
You can leave rainy London and go to the sun.
You can leave your boring class
And even zoom past
Saturn, Jupiter or even Mars.

But when you awake from this starry night
Then you discover a disappointing sight
No more spaceship, space or Mars
No more looking at the shooting stars
Instead you see your mum shaking you
And telling you what to do.

You pull yourself out of your sleep
And go to brush your teeth,
You trip over your shoe
As you go to the loo.

'Stop daydreaming,' cries Mum.

Daisy Kirtley (12)
Lycée Français Charles de Gaulle

I Have A Dream

I hate French lessons in general,
They are even worse on a wet, cold Friday afternoon,
When I could be in the French Alps staring at the moon.
Unluckily, I am still in the stuffy French classroom.

I have a dream.

I wish I was on a nice slope in Meribel,
There is one word to describe school, it has to be 'torture.'
They are doing it on purpose, I am sure!

I have a dream.

I would much prefer to be in the French mountains,
Where I could drink from fountains.
I would be able to ski, enjoy myself and sledge,
As the chalet we're staying in has the cutting edge.

I have a dream.

As it happens, I've been dog-marched into maths,
Luckily, I'll soon be on a brilliant French slope.
Now I am counting the hours
Until the chalet will be ours.

I have a dream.

Luke Robinson (11)
Lycée Français Charles de Gaulle

I Have A Dream

I have a dream that every kid,
Can have the chance that I did,
Learn to write, read and play,
They all deserve these each day.

Every morning I wake up and say:
'What new things will I learn today?'
English? Maths? French or history?
Whatever it is it will be helping me.

Education is a huge part of school,
Even though it ain't always cool,
For my future it is very important,
That I work hard to find my talent.

My friends, I will keep them forever,
They are so nice, caring and clever.
We have fun, play and laugh together,
And we are always there for each other.

You may think of school as buildings,
Yet for us children it is much more.
We come to share thoughts and feelings,
In this place called school that we adore.

Liliane Momeni (11)
Lycée Français Charles de Gaulle

I Have A Dream

I have a dream
Of changing people's lives,
Yes!
And that's through TV.

I have a dream
Of helping people through hard times,
Making sure everyone in the whole world
Knows that someone else miserable.

I have a dream
Of sharing people's points of view,
Without arguing
And with respect.

I have a dream
Of arresting crimes,
Showing to the world
How humans can be sickening.

And that's all by being an actress.
TV explains to everyone
In every language
Who we are.

Julie Le Gall (12)
Lycée Français Charles de Gaulle

I Have a Dream . . .

Imagine a world made of sweets . . .
It should be nice to eat!
Imagine . . .
Imagine money growing in trees . . .
There won't be any bees!
Imagine . . .
Imagine you just have friends . . .
Then friendship will have no end!
Imagine . . .
Imagine for there just to be sun . . .
That would be so much fun!
Imagine . . .
Imagine no war . . .
No one would be sore!
Imagine . . .
Imagine no rules . . .
Or maybe even pools!
Imagine . . .
Imagine all these things becoming true . . .
Just imagine . . .

Eléonore Bacher (11)
Lycée Français Charles de Gaulle

I Have A Dream

Just inside of me,
I have a dream,
Like a bird has a song to sing,
A thought locked inside of me . . .

I have a dream,
That angels can fly,
That children can play,
And everything's right,
For me to say . . .

I have a dream,
That I can fly,
That I can play,
That I am everything
I say . . .

I have a dream,
That the time is right
For me to make this dream
Become . . . reality . . .

Matthieu Lange (11)
Lycée Français Charles de Gaulle

I Have A Dream

I have a dream. One day, child labour will be abolished.

I have a dream. One day, I can sleep a whole night.

I have a dream. One day, poverty will disappear,
And wealth and fortune will appear in my country and family.

I have a dream. One day, my parents will be waiting for me.

I have a dream. One day, my master will stop whipping me
And respect me.

I have a dream. One day, all my dreams will come true.

Dany Oueini (13)
Lycée Français Charles de Gaulle

I Have A Dream

Imagine a place after tomorrow,
There would be no war, no death,
Or even a threat.
I have a dream.
Imagine a tree with money
Imagine Superman was real
All I want is peace . . .
I have a dream.
Imagine somewhere,
Somewhere special
Where only I could go
I have a dream.
Imagine far away
A place for me to stay
Somebody to look after me
Somebody to rescue me
I have a dream.

Charlotte Baines (11)
Lycée Français Charles de Gaulle

School

Why do children have to go to school?
Why can't they go to pools?
At school children sleep
While their parents weep with pity.

School compared to a pool will never rule
Because when kids are at school they're in pain
But out of school they could be in the hall of fame.

Tests, tests, tests, tests, tests
Children get pest from tests
Oh! That reminds me
I have a test!

Houston Parke (11)
Lycée Français Charles de Gaulle

I Have A Dream

I have a dream;
That the world is upside down.
That big means small,
That werewolves are going to the ball.
That cats are afraid of mice,
That trolls are nice.

I have a dream;
Of a school without homework,
Of lesson without words.
That classrooms are playgrounds,
That teachers are students;
That class bells are beautiful songs.

When I woke up this morning,
I saw cats running, chasing mice;
I saw my homework on my desk . . .
And I knew it was just one dream.

Mathilde Coutte (11)
Lycée Français Charles de Gaulle

Tired On My Bed

After this rough journey,
I lay tired on my disarranged bed.

I'm thinking of my life,
I'm thinking of my master who is spiteful.

I'm thinking of my health,
Which is unfortunately not promising.

I'm thinking of my friends,
Who are happy living with their family.

I'm thinking of myself,
A seven-year-old child, working as . . . a slave.

Philippine Christolomme (14)
Lycée Français Charles de Gaulle

Reality

I saw my parents,
Their kind smiles.
I saw my brothers and sisters,
Their games and their jokes.
I saw the house,
With the beds on the floor.
I saw the village,
Crossed by the river.
The water turned green, scales, fangs and cruel eyes appeared.
The snake stared at me, peering in my head through my eyes.
He said: 'Forget them, I bought you. Freedom does not exist.'

I woke up, completely panicked.
My face was wet . . .
Was it sweat or was it the water from the river?
Was it tears or was it venom?
I started to cry.

Charlotte Gallice (13)
Lycée Français Charles de Gaulle

I Have A Dream

I have a dream
I would be a sun,
If I am the sun, I shine in the day,
But I am the moon,
I shine at night,
With my friends the stars.
In my dream,
I am beautiful,
I am big and I have respect.
I dance and I sing every day,
But I awake and I think of my dream.
My friend the star, Lili, says to me:
'If you were the sun, you would be the moon.'

Julie Penverne (11)
Lycée Français Charles de Gaulle

I Have A Dream

Imagine a world ravaged by war
Imagine never-ending poverty and death
But soon we will no longer need to imagine such things
For they will be real very soon.

I have a dream

A dream that would save our world if realised
Imagine the end of all wars
Imagine prosperity and long life
Imagine that dream realised.

But these things will not be easy
We will have to make many sacrifices
Not by ourselves, but as a race
We will have to help each other as one
And then we will be truly prosperous and happy.

Matthew Conradi (11)
Lycée Français Charles de Gaulle

I Have A Dream

I have always lived in poverty,
Working as a slave every day isn't easy,

The conditions of work are dreadful,
Sometimes the master whips you as if you were an animal,

You have only one hope, that is called liberty,
And you envy the children who are free,

You never get a chance to play,
And have to work all day,

Without cheap labour
Europeans wouldn't have any sweaters,

Unfortunately this is how my life goes,
Tears for some and laughter for others.

Manon Rouzé (13)
Lycée Français Charles de Gaulle

I Have A Dream

When your puberty comes,
You want to be free,
All those children do
But they cannot be.

School is their dreams,
School is their life.
They know what it means,
Who'll accept being their wife?

Can we do anything for them?
Will they have any future?
Can they stop taking them?
Is slavery against human nature?
That is the question.

Quentin Santucci (13)
Lycée Français Charles de Gaulle

I Have A Dream

When I grow up, I want to be a baker.
I'd wake up early in the morning,
But it won't be for the same thing!
I could make a chocolate cake or a strawberry pie,
But at least, I am sure I won't die!
I wonder if cheesecake is really made with cheese . . .
But even if it isn't, I am sure I will not get any disease.
What about a pancake with maple syrup?
Because here, in the factory, no one even knows the taste of a lollipop.
Perhaps an apple crumble?
Because that won't make me tremble!
Anyway, I don't care if I am just a factory worker,
I hope my life will soon get better.

Clara Tourme (13)
Lycée Français Charles de Gaulle

95

I Had A Dream

I visited Africa
Especially in Nigeria
I saw children
Who were treated like chickens
There was no school
No swimming pool
They had no money
So they lived in poverty
Their masters were so scary
That the children were unhappy
In this big factory.

Diego De Liedekerke (14)
Lycée Français Charles de Gaulle

I Have A Dream . . .

I have a dream . . .
I dreamt I was free,
I dreamt I was like any other child,
I dreamt I was with my family,
I dreamt I could live like any other child,
I dreamt I could do what I wanted to,
I dreamt my parents were still alive,
I dreamt about something I could do,
I dreamt I world dive
In a pool of freedom.

Sacha Cohen-Scali (13)
Lycée Français Charles de Gaulle

I Have A Dream

I have a dream,
That there is world peace,
No hunger,
Clean water,
And a home for everyone.

Release the innocent,
Heal the sick,
Give food to the hungry,
Give drink to the thirsty,
Free the oppressed,
Let the deaf hear,
Let the blind see,
Comfort the upset.

Let no family be divorced,
And everyone
Love each other.
And death shall flee,
And life shall rule
Forever.

Archie Philipps (12)
Lyndhurst House Preparatory School

I Have A Dream

I have a dream
That the light will beam.
I want to hear the waves crashing
Not cars bashing.
My mum is sad
When the environment is so bad.
It is unfair
Getting a roar like a flare.

Humphrey Stanton-Ife (10)
Lyndhurst House Preparatory School

I Have A Dream

I have a dream to live my life well.
To work hard and have a family.
I have a dream to change the world
To make a difference.
I have a dream to walk on the slick red carpet of fame
And not to lose myself.
I have a dream to make the world a better place
To stop poverty and cruelty.
I have a dream to bash a hundred runs at Lords
To become a great sporting hero.
I have a dream to make the world green
To recycle and clean.
My name is Henry
And I have a dream.

Henry Somper (11)
Lyndhurst House Preparatory School

Nature's Dream

I dream that I can hear the birds singing
Everywhere I go
That there are animals
Everywhere I go
That there are no roads
Just forests, mountains and wildlife
Just think about it for a moment
Think what the world would look like
Think that there would be no car fumes
No pollution
No big cities, just towns and villages
Wouldn't that be lovely?
That is my dream
What is yours?

Cameron Burt (10)
Lyndhurst House Preparatory School

No Dream Is Too Big

Dreams are fantastic, dreams make people happy,
I have dreams, for education, my family,
I'd give anything for my family,
I would be a musician, an actor, an author,
But no one knows what the future can hold,
My main dreams are for health, education, success,
Wealth, I want to have good friends,
A good wife,
Most definitely, my family,
For peace,
Who said you can't dream big
No dream is too . . . big!

Gazi Cokay (10)
Lyndhurst House Preparatory School

A New Way

A dream has come true
Obama is new
The truth looks strange
Everything is going to change
No more war
A better law
No differences of race
In spite of colour of one's face.

Torin Francis (12)
Lyndhurst House Preparatory School

My World

M y world would be as good as gold, where nobody grows old!
Y ou would have so much fun, since nobody is really that dumb

W ish you can join me in this world, I guarantee you it's just gold
O r just want a good life, well my world has no strife
R eally it's where you want to be, because everybody is no different to me
L ife can never get better, since nothing is truly better
D on't you wish this would be real? So come and join me in my dream.

Fauzi Alhakmi (10)
Lyndhurst House Preparatory School

Dreams

I magine difference
M e, you can change it all
A dream
G enerations
I nspiration
N ow
E veryone.

Philip Kaczmarczyk (12)
Lyndhurst House Preparatory School

I Have A Dream

Imagine an imaginary world
Where you can make your dream come true
And nothing can stop you from getting what you want
And you don't need to fight for it
And you will have all you ever wanted
And make life come in peace.

Bose Jimoh (13)
Prendergast Ladywell Fields College

Imagine

Imagine an imaginary world where you can be
Anything you want to be.

And where you won't get hurt
And where there are all types of creatures
And there are demons
And you can fly in the sky
And you can be powerful.

That is the world that I would choose to create
Because it is big

And there is peace
And happiness
And there are all types of life living together.

Zeki Tacsoy (13)
Prendergast Ladywell Fields College

Imagine

Imagine a world where you can be anything you want to be.
Where you can go fishing
And where you can go playing with your friends,
And you can fly in the sky.
And where you can go to school.
And where you can go to work.
That is the world that I would choose to create
Because it is nice.
And no one can get hit
And people are happy
And people can live together.

Oak Srisarakham (14)
Prendergast Ladywell Fields College

Imaginary World

Imagine an imaginary world where you can drive a floating car.
And there is more time to play games and watch TV.
And there is more Mother Nature that surrounds us.
And peace for everyone
And you can speak to animals.
That is the world that I would choose to create
Because it has mostly what people need.
And people will feel safe
And learn more about Mother nature.
And it is a life that people would like to live.

Ziahyel Hodge (13)
Prendergast Ladywell Fields College

Imagine . . . Me Being The President Of The USA

Racing in my Porsche
Flying in my private jet
Driving in my Porsche
Swimming in my blue and gold pool
Beat-boxing in my mansion
Rapping in my studio
Playing with my son and daughter
Running in my garden.

Charlie Huckle (14)
Prendergast Ladywell Fields College

I Have A Dream

Many years ago there was a great man with a dream
Who fought for rights and no segregation
Now it's my turn to share my dream
To cities, towns and every nation.

I have a dream . . .

The lovely motherland continents would arise
Instead of being poor and terrorised
Africa, where nature takes place
Would also be a happier and better race.

I have a dream . . .

The children of Africa would have better education
Instead of no food and starvation
The sick and needy shall be healed
Because the viruses and bacteria will be killed.

I have a dream . . .

Bang! The sound of a gunshot
Happening on the streets of South East
My dream is to stop all the commotion
It's causing our society a lot of emotion
A lot of children getting shot every week
More new victims the fools will seek
Young little boys dying at the age of ten
Didn't even make it to be young men
The bullet of the gun crashed through the heart to meet
As the poor little boys fell to their feet
The mothers of the boys have to go through the pain
So why put them through all that strain?
Being a criminal is not cool
So drop the guns and don't be a fool.

I have a dream . . .

Carbon dioxide filling the air
But still no one takes the time to care
If only someone could listen and be seated
From there my dream will be almost completed
Vans, trucks, cars beware

When eco-people figure out something you can't bear
The planet will be a proud and successful place
No pollution, acid rain or foul air
Together we can make a better planet and care.

I have a dream . . .

The prayers of a young child will be heard
Her mother, father will never touch her
To this I will never sleep
Until my speech is kept to keep
The violence, betrayal is all over
The child will grow up peaceful, no lies
Never would she know about hurt again
She will no longer have problems or pain.

I have a dream . . .

The wrong doings of her father and mother
Don't worry, the girl will be safe, as well as her brother.
They'll keep on going, no longer be afraid
Since they'll have God in them, they'll be saved.

I have a dream . . .

Together we can make this dream happen,
We will stand tall
But if we stay apart and divided,
We will just fall

I have a dream . . .

Comfort Hassan (14)
SS Saviour's & Olave's School, Southwark

I Have A Dream . . .

I have a dream,
A dream that every human will wake up light-headed
With visions of achievement, promise and reward.
To a world that lives together in perfect conformity.

I have a dream today.

I have a dream, a dream that every nation will live in perfect harmony
Instead of the loud bombardment of guns and bombs
We will have the tranquillity of the beautiful human race.

I have a dream today.

A dream when if we stand together we can make a change
That will impact the way we see life,
The way we love, because we are all looking for something.
There can be a life without venom and annoyance.

I have a dream today.

Instead if the sounds of fear in screams
And the hurried pace of running from death,
The scream of delight as people laugh and run, full of life.
Indisputably, we can make this change for the good.

I have a dream today.

Where the little boys and girls will be smothered with devotion and
leadership
From mothers and fathers.
There will be no gun and knife crime as a consequence of absent fathers
Instead young men will be striving towards success
Pushed by the presence of a father figure.

I have a dream today.

A dream, a vision, a new future, where peace will conquer all,
Peacefully, equally and with justice
And instead of people filled with venomous anger
Their cups will overflow with joy.

This is my dream today!

Christina Walker (14)
SS Saviour's & Olave's School, Southwark

I Have A Dream . . .

I have a dream . . .
I'm the most handsome male,
I have bulging abs,
I'm 10 on the sexy scale.

I have a dream . . .
All the girls love me,
All the boys are jealous of me,
How easy can this be?

I have a dream . . .
I left the glasses behind,
I'm the best at sport,
And I can bump and grind.

I have a dream . . .
Girls are the heart and I'm the key,
This is so corny,
Don't you wish you were me?

I have a dream . . .
This will become real,
But this is my dream,
So don't steal what I feel.

Lola Ogunrinde (15)
SS Saviour's & Olave's School, Southwark

I Have A Dream

I have a dream
That water will be provided all over the world
North, east, south and west.

I have a dream
That Africa's poorest will have water and be blessed
North, east, south and west.

I have a dream
That water can be available anyhow and anywhere
North, south, east and west.

If the universe is made up of 80% water and 20% land
Why is 20% land suffering when there's 80% water?

I have a dream
That water will be provided all over the world
Do you have a dream?

Bliss Moukoko (15)
SS Saviour's & Olave's School, Southwark

Believer

Believe that your voice can change the world
Believe that small actions can make a big difference.
Believe that *believers* can make that change
Believe that you can stop poverty, war, racism and discrimination.
Believe that you could stop hatred and pain
Believe that *believers* can make that change
Believe that we all can live in peace.
Believe that you can mend the world with your words.
Believe that *believers* can make that change
Believe that all it takes is words stronger than a bullet or a sword
Believe that you're that believer that
Makes *that change!*

Rebecca Bada (13)
St Angela's Ursuline Convent School, Forest Gate

Diversion Of The Mind

Isn't it funny how
The touch of a cool page beneath my fingertips
Is the touch of love itself?
Funny
How every line engraves its meaning
Into my head.
Strange. How each chapter spurs such emotions
Unbeknownst to my knowledge.

The words are theatre to my mind
Where I am the actress.
A sweet disturbance to my thoughts
A haven for my troubled soul
Where havoc surrounds me,
But
Unable to harm me in my nirvana of literature.
For Shakespeare reminds me that I can love,
Walker reassures me of my strength
Within my race and within my sex.
Angelou shows me that still I rise
And although I rise
I fall
As the poetic wall I have built around me
Crumbles
Like the neglected hardbacks of yesterday.

Isn't it funny how
All I read, is all I see
In a world where ignorance
Is all we feel?

Natasha Mwansa (16)
St Angela's Ursuline Convent School, Forest Gate

Me And My Memories

I reach the sky
Play with clouds
Sit with the flowers
Hold hands with the sun
Here comes reality check

I land

It hurts but Earth isn't that bad
There comes a time where
Every angel has to fall
When I fell
They called it my birthday

I seek to smile
I love to laugh
Hitherto I have no reason to

Perhaps tomorrow I can go back and
Play with the clouds
Sit with the flowers
Hold hands with the sun
Then tomorrow I won't break hearts

It may be a nightmare
I pinch myself
Ouch . . . I felt that
The nightmare called reality.

I long to be in the sky again
To be with clouds the flowers the sun
The clouds never stay
The flowers die away
The sun is too far away

I see the clouds I tiptoe
I can't touch you
Let alone play
I see the flowers here
Look at them
I look at me
I look away

I spot the sun
I reach out my hands
That's only when you choose to come
I'm told I can't touch you
They told me you'll kill me
So I stay absent from your presence

What happened to the love we had
The jokes we told
The memories we stored

No one remembers the flowers
Neither the clouds nor the sun
People call it moving on
I'll try to go on

Forgetting memories
Is something I cannot do but every day
I try to dream of something else
To forget my forgotten past
When I know clearly
Memories are all I will ever leave behind.

Angelie Samuel (15)
St Angela's Ursuline Convent School, Forest Gate

Words Of A Rose

I am a flourishing rose
Hated by all, confronted by few
Despised because of the inferiority of my petals
And the stabbing pain of my thorns.

They cause pain
Anguish,
Suffering,
Torment,
Distress,
Not of which I caused
But by the sharpness of the other roses.

They loathe my appearance
With every passing moment.
They see no likeness,
No resemblance with their beings
I am looked upon with such brutality and inhumanity.

I am looked upon with twisted faces
Faces of anger and detestation
They spit at my every word
At my every suggestion they snort.
Even the sound of my breath
They hate!
I am unique, I am beautiful
My thorns are sharp
So what?
I love to live and I live to love.

I am different but the same
I stand up and speak up, for what I believe
Smiling is my game
I am the change I want to see in my world

So what if I am different
Aren't I still not a rose?

There's violence in our world
People killing, people dying
People hurting, see them crying
You've got to stand up, speak up
For what you believe . . .

Maureen Lum (14)
St Angela's Ursuline Convent School, Forest Gate

I Have Dreams . . .

I am going to be on top of the world soon enough,
Maybe even literally.
I'll be living in the luxurious penthouse apartments of New York City,
Just streets away from the headquarters of my multi-million dollar
fashion label -
The fashion label of all things fly - fun and glamorous.
Yes, this successful clothing line
Founded by my good friend and soon to be business partner,
Tia-Rose and myself.
We plan to bring even more flavour to the world of fashion
And inspire young models and designers to do more with their
opportunities.

Personally however, when it comes to changing the world, I want to
do more.
It might be directing, producing, writing and even starring in
Touching and entertaining films, or documentaries that show how life
Affects different people.
I have even started to think about photography,
And how I see the world.
There is so much to do in life, yet so little time to do it,
Which is why some of you reading this may feel my aspirations
Are either too high or unrealistic.
But answer me this question:

Why don't you think I can make it?

The only person to stop you doing something is you.

Jennelle Reece-Gardner (14)
St Martin-in-the-Fields High School for Girls, Lambeth

I Have A Dream Of A Better Place

I have a dream of a better place
The whole world covered in every race
Violent kids, at the end of the street
Misled children, many cliques
Many parents led astray
Too many children taken away
Guns and knives found in pockets
Bags of weed, buckets and buckets
Lots of waste thrown on the ground
Not a bit of clean ground around
Young children having babies
Too busy to rest.
Have we pushed our parents too far?
Put them to the test?
They always tried to show you right,
But you never listened.
And, Mum always said to you,
'Your future will surely glisten.'
You used to lift your head up high,
Now you just feel guilt inside.
What could we do to change the world?
It could take one little girl
So, next time when you're acting silly in class
Just think about your future
I have a dream of a better place!
So go and get an A* in maths
Because you're in charge of changing the world
Have fun in life, be sure about what you do.
I have a dream of a better place
And we need the help of *you.*

Kamesha Adamson (13)
St Martin-in-the-Fields High School for Girls, Lambeth

You Can Do Anything If You Try

'Stay in school, don't you slack
You have to work harder because you're black.'
This is something my grandmother would say
She would nag me about it every day.

It's very true, I shouldn't slack
But it shouldn't only be because I'm black
Black and white should love one another
Live together and care for each other.

You can be anything if you try
Just do your best and aim high
A dancer, a teacher, a very caring nurse
Concentrate in school and you'll come first.

I aim to go to a good uni
And become a lawyer, because I have the opportunity
I hope to earn lots of money
And to have someone to call me honey.

Only four kids, not any more
They'll go to school and get high scores
They'll work very hard, and I'll be proud to see
That they'll be very successful, *just like me!*

You can be anything, if you try
Just give it a go, and aim high.

Ramatta Saffie Conteh (14)
St Martin-in-the-Fields High School for Girls, Lambeth

My Dreams

My dreams are,
To tour across the British Channel,
Search for gold at the end of the rainbow,
And to roll down the green hills of Wales.

To see,
The icy lands of Antarctica
Myself waving to a crowd on television.
And to see a tall dinosaur eating crunchy leaves.

To hear,
The loud screeching of the dinosaurs while they're being hunted,
My songs being played on the radio,
And to hear the baby monkeys scream.

To feel,
The long spotted neck of a giraffe,
The soft wet head of a dolphin,
And to feel the crystal-blue Atlantic Ocean.

To smell,
The sweet scent of coconut water,
The tropical aroma of tropical fruits,
And to smell the lovely perfume that my mummy wears.

To taste,
The juicy tropical fruits that my uncle picks,
The delicious sour sop punch my grandmother makes,
And to taste the mouthwatering breadfruit my daddy makes.

And my wildest dream is to reach for the stars!

Riann Brown (12)
St Paul's Academy, Plumstead

I Have A Dream

When I grow up, I want to achieve power to change the world.
I will stop all that's bad and begin all that's good.

When I grow up, I want to achieve power to change the world
I will tackle terrible terrorism
And stop burglary from taking over.

When I grow up, I want to achieve power to change the world.
I will create a camp where people can go to learn how to defend
themselves.
It will be a necessity.

When I grow up I want to achieve the power to change the world.
I will stop the Credit Crunch by making people stop spending
Too much money and this will go on and on.

When I grow up I want to achieve the power to change the world.
I will make overweight children and adults (not to be rude)
Go to the gyms I set up.

When I grow up I want to achieve the power to change the world.
I will stop global warming,
I will work with the world leaders, and . . .

I will go on and on,
All I want to do is change the world.
Then I will retire in a retirement home, in Italy.

Prince Ofoegbu
St Paul's Academy, Plumstead

The King's Dream

If I were king for one day
I would clean all the mess away
Make this town shine because it would be mine
But that would never happen
And this is just a dream,
So it seems.

Joshu Atuhutra (12)
St Paul's Academy, Plumstead

I Have A Dream - The Best Footballer That Ever Lived

When the players run fast,
I'm going to run faster,
When the players are skilful,
I'm going to be more skilful.

I'm the best footballer that ever lived.

When the players want the ball,
I want it more,
When players go in for a 50-50 tackle,
I'm going to go in harder.

I'm the best footballer that ever lived.

When the players jump for a header,
I'm going to jump higher,
When players are passing it well,
I'm going to pass it better.
Whatever a player does,
I'm going to do it better.

Because I'm the best footballer that ever lived.

Kieran McMahon (12)
St Paul's Academy, Plumstead

I Have A Dream

I tossed and turned awaiting the wonder of dream to take me away,
I lay on my side underneath my volcanic duvet slowly drifting away.

The weight of my eyelids dragged me away to an unknown place.
My iron will forced me to my feet, I heard a familiar voice,
My feet swivelled around and a smile spread across my face
I was discombobulated, my old friends I wanted to hug
But I stopped myself because I know a dream's a dream
And that's all it will be.

Joseph Mannah
St Paul's Academy, Plumstead

I Have A Dream

I have a dream that I am the king of the world
My people they listen
They don't say a word.

My first rule is no one will hate in my world
Everything is great
Also there will be no bad
So nobody will ever be sad.

My second rule is no guns, no fighting, no violence!
Or you might get a court sentence.

My third rule is I would have scientists searching for cures
Also it would be good if we could become faster,
Stronger, younger, older like superheroes.

My fourth and final rule is
Everyone will be equal
Children and adults.

I will be a king that listens,
Trustworthy and most of all kind
And that is my dream . . .

Temitope Odusanwo (11)
St Paul's Academy, Plumstead

Untitled

I did have a dream, the kind
Of dream like being president
Or a great doctor
But that is not a dream I want.

A dream is something that is personal to you,
Something that only you can complete.
That you can only depend on yourself.

But it is super difficult in
This society to create this dream.
With all the talk of death and suicide,
Bombs around in our world destroying it like a squash of a bug.
Can be stepped on by the foot of authority.

One of my dreams is to make other people's dreams come true,
So while you are reading this think of yours
And it just might come true.

I have a dream that is personal to me:
How about you?

Martha Lucas (16)
St Paul's Academy, Plumstead

Chocolate Dream

Chocolate, chocolate
Wonderful chocolate
Astonishing in the photos
Sensational in my mind
What will I do without you?

Chocolate, chocolate
Beautiful chocolate
Lovely and juicy in my mouth
Extraordinary like a butterfly in my hand
If only I knew what it will be in my stomach.

Wasil Mousavi
St Paul's Academy, Plumstead

119

I Have A Dream

I will come
Into school with
The funkiest haircut
And no one will laugh at me . . .

I will say anything without people
Saying anything bad about me.

I have a dream
That I can dance
Like Chris Brown
And have more friends
Than I can imagine.

I have a dream that
I can play like Ronaldinho
And play for the school football team
And play every time.

I have a dream
That I am the next Martin Luther King.

Machindo Mwambazi (12)
St Paul's Academy, Plumstead

My Money Dream

First I was poor, now I am rich
All because of that one chip
Should I put it on black or red
Or on my
Birthday number
22? Should
I put on £100 - £1000
Or 1 mile or should I throw
It up in the
Air?

George O'Grady
St Paul's Academy, Plumstead

Becoming A Teen Sensation!

I would just wake up in the morning
With my chef in my room with my breakfast ready on my front desk.
'Oh my wonders!' Of being a star
Then I would go round in my Lamborghini car.

I've dreamt about this day since I was a little kid
The next day I couldn't believe the things I then did.
I sang like an angel, I danced like a butterfly,
I jumped and flew to all kinds of music,
I performed like a star, I never knew I could do it.

I had thought in my mind, of a person who had been my idol for years,
She's pretty, she's sweet she can never put you to tears.
If I met her today I would stand on my bed jumping up and down
                                          upon my head.

If I could really dream of the boys who really influence me to sing
                                          and use my talent,
I would cry and sigh for meeting the Jonas Brothers eye to eye.
'Oh my wonders,' I can dream I love my future life forever.

Tammy Osara-Osaghae
St Paul's Academy, Plumstead

I Had A Dream

Once I had a dream
I dreamt I was a king
And all the other kings and queens
They were not better than me.
Because they were all adults
And I was just a kid.
But because I was so good
I ruled the world
I got rid of all the guns and knives
And all the people who take other people's lives.

Kyle Murphy (13)
St Paul's Academy, Plumstead

121

My Childhood Dream

I'm going to tell you my childhood dream,
To have a room coloured with cream.
A balcony that is big and wide,
With a long, crazy, yellow slide.
A bedroom the size of the grand hall,
With giant, tall, bright blue walls.
A bed so big that it fits 10 princesses,
With a wardrobe with 1000 dresses.
A mirror that can show my full image,
A bird that can send out my messages.
To have a garden filled with trees,
Like a forest filled with leaves.
A water fountain as big as the house,
Or a waterfall that could display the clouds.
For a pet I would like a tiger or dragon
Something like that to show my passion.
A crazy thought when I was watching the sun,
But it was my dream since I was young.

Nhien Kieu Le
St Paul's Academy, Plumstead

I Have A Dream

I have a dream and I believe.
Hold your head high when it seems dark
Then you'll be reaching for that shining star.
Imagine all things are possible, if you only just believe.

I have a dream and I believe.
I will survive and grow. For God has told me so.
Imagine all things are possible, if you only just believe.

I have a dream and I believe.
There will be hope and peace one day.
Imagine all things are possible if you only just believe.

I have a dream and I believe.
We, the world, will be finished with our hatred and filled with only
gentle touching love.
Imagine all things are possible, if you only just believe.

Sophia Pham (12)
St Paul's Academy, Plumstead

I Have A Dream

I have a dream
My dream is to play for
Manchester United Football Club.

I was dreaming in bed
I was training with Man United players.

Everyone went to the changing room.
Screaming, shouting, laughing and fighting.
Not a real fight, a play fight.

Sir Alex came and said
'I'm starting,'
I said, 'Starting what?'
'Starting the pop,' Sir Alex said.
Everyone was laughing.

Pascal Zoil (12)
St Paul's Academy, Plumstead

I Have A Dream

I have a dream that I have super powers.
If I had super powers I would have laser vision.
I would save the day every day.

There would be no mugging and fighting
Only when I saved people.
I would be a great role model to everyone
And they would want to become like me.

I wouldn't have policemen doing their jobs because I would.
I would save the world.
The power that I would have would be to fly right to the sky,
Super strength, heat ray.
Which I could use night and day.

I have a dream that I have super powers.

Raphael President (11)
St Paul's Academy, Plumstead

If I Ruled The Sheep

If I ruled the sheep,
I'd make some changes fast,
Everyone would stop eating lamb

And mutton too.

If I ruled the sheep,
I'd get rid of all the mean farmers,
Everyone would love the sheep,

And the lambs.

What did the lambs and sheep,
Ever do to you?
Why eat them?

Niamh Douglas
St Paul's Academy, Plumstead

If I Ruled The World

If I ruled the world, things would be different,
No war, no more mourning for the brave
Love, peace and harmony,
There would be kindness and joyfulness
Will stand by me.

If I ruled the world,
No more gas-powered cars
Electrical and friendly for our needs
Global warming slowed down,
There would be ball games in the street
20mph would be the speed limit
I wish I could rule the world.

Hayden Cottrell
St Paul's Academy, Plumstead

I Have A Dream

I have a dream . . .
A life to live.
A dream to dream.
A sleep to sleep.
A talk to talk.

This is my dream,
My man to meet,
I don't know who,
But he, my story and life,
To find and understand.

I have a dream . . .
A life to live.
A dream to dream.
A sleep to sleep.
A talk to talk.

And a future to fulfil.

Millie Campanale (13)
The Arts Educational School

Petronella

I can't stop thinking about her.

It started when I joined the school,
They were the rulers, I was the fool.
I wished for make-up, iPods too!
Designer gear, always new.
I dreamt of sleepovers, shared secrets and shopping,
Special favour.

Last night, I had another dream.
She wasn't smiling, not one beam.
Her face was contorted with rage.
As I stared,
Even more she glared.
Before me stood a hideous creature,
Her body the sample of some terrible feature,
Hairy, bloody, claws muddy.
And then I saw what I had become,
A puppet in need of some . . .
Love? Admiration? What was it I wanted?

Before I met Petra I was a sensible girl,
I didn't force my hair to curl.
I got top marks in every test,
Played in the parks and all the rest.
Then, just to please her,
I stopped maths with Head Sir.
Now look where I am - a hairdresser,
How glam.

Memories carry me through the sky,
All of this, one big lie.
Yeah, sure, she was my friend,
How can my heart ever mend?
I thought she was my soul,
Now I am so cold.

Petra,
Petronella Werewolf
My friend.

Marie Claire de Voil (11)
The Arts Educational School

They're Teenagers

They walk around with guns, they say, they walk around with knives.
They run around, shouting names at all the passers-by. They're laughing at
The cripple. Laughing at the poor. Acting all like chavs. Laughing at you all.
They're all getting pregnant. They're all taking drugs. They're all smoking
Weed. They're all killing thugs. They run around your neighbourhood,
Smashing up our car. Breaking into houses. Going way too far. But . . . are
We really like that?
Are we even sane? Are
We going crazy? Like
Terrorists on a
Plane. Cos, really we're not
Like that. Really
We're quite sweet.
Some of us are
Crazy. But not all
Of us are freaks.
We don't all walk
Around with guns.
We shout back. And
We don't all walk
Around with knives!
Only some of us shout at
All the passers-by. We're
Not all getting pregnant
We're not all taking drugs
We're not all smoking weed.

And we're

Definitely

Not

Killing thugs.

Antonia Blakeman (14)
The Arts Educational School

127

She Has A Dream

She has a dream.
A dream to meet,
Someone special.
Every night she dreams
To meet her father.

It would be her dream come true,
To hold her father,
To kiss her father
And to meet her father.
Once.

She has a dream,
To see him
And to be with him.

In her dream she looks
She searches and searches
For her father, dad.
In her dream she's angry,
Why, why did he leave her?
She wasn't even born.
She hates him so much.

She has a dream
To hit him,
To shout and scream.
She does not like him
She loves him.

Arthur Williams (14)
The Arts Educational School

I Have A Dream

I have a dream,
Of a better world,
A world of no evil doing,
And a world of love and peace.

I dream of a cleaner world,
A world of no pollution,
A land of greener country,
With freedom for animals and humans.

I dream of a freer world,
A world of people doing their own will,
A land of animals grazing freely,
A free country and community.

I dream of a crime-free world,
A world of no violence,
A land of no disagreement,
And of peace and goodwill.

I dream of a connected world,
A world of people talking,
A land of humans communicating,
And of people rejoicing.

I dream of a nation
Sharing its thoughts and feelings.
I dream of a community
That will unite as one.

Brogan Webber (12)
The Arts Educational School

I Have A Dream

I have a dream.
Not to change the world
Or have world peace or domination,

But to love myself,
My friends, my family,
And to love my country, my nation.

I have a dream,
Yes, to stop crime
But that's not my main priority,

I want to never upset
Any friend again,
Well, that's in the minority.

But I do have one dream,
A very important one too,
To stop hatred, no more murders.

And I hope that the human nation,
Like me,
Will have a dream and go further.

Eve Burns (13)
The Arts Educational School

I Wish

I close my eyes,
And then I wake up
But I'm not in my bed
And the sun is up.
I'm not in London,
Paris
Or Rome
But I'm inside my head
And it feels like home.
There is something bulky,
Inside my pocket.
My hand reaches in, it's a beautiful locket.
Cute boy struts past,
I pant very slowly.
My breath smells of fresh mint,
If only, if only.
Loud noise is ringing,
Sweat on my palm,
My eyes open wide,
Drat, the alarm!

Mei Borg-Cardona (12)
The Arts Educational School

I Have A Dream . . .

I have a dream to fly high in the sky
Dance all over the world and
Swim in lots of money.

I want to own a shopping mall
I want to meet big stars
I want pixies, unicorns and
Mermaids to be real.

I also have a dream to have powers that
No one knows about
Own big houses around the world and
No more global warming.

Whitney Svosve (11)
The Arts Educational School

Bunking School

Our parents send us to school every day
But how do they know I go astray?
Why did I follow my friend
When there is school I could attend?
I'm nearly 16 and it ain't very funny
I realised I won't get a job or earn money
I should have gone to school to learn
And now money I can't even earn
It is very important to go to school
Don't be like me and be a fool
Now I've lost my chance to earn money
Don't copy me because it ain't very funny.
I've learnt my lesson and now it's too late
I now know that I have met my fate
So when your parents send you to school
Don't act like me and be a fool!

Victoria Jordan (11)
Turin Grove School

Black, White, Red And Blue

Black, white, red and blue
They're just colours too
Why the need to hate?
Just because of one's race,
They feel the urge to discriminate
But really they're just a disgrace.

Black, white, red and blue
They're just colours too
There is no such thing as a person white as a winter's snow
Nor black as the burning charcoal.
Racism should be in the past, from time ago
They're just words, which are taken beyond control.

Black, white, red and blue
They're just colours too
There is no need for the racist remarks
We are all equal, we have the same rights
Such simple words can cause sparks
Just like how a fire ignites.

Black, white, red and blue
They're just colours too
We are one, we are a nation
There should be harmony and peace
We are the next generation
Where racism will decease.

Black, white, red and blue
They're just colours too
What is racism?
Segregating someone because of their complexion?
Which is the truth and realism
Or believing that you are superior to a different race person?
Rather than hate we should show affection.

Black, white, red and blue
They're just colours too
Why the need to hate
Just because of one's race?
They feel the rage to discriminate
But really they're just a disgrace.

Mellissa Walker (14)
Turin Grove School

Colours Of The Heart

Anger is red,
Jealousy is green,
Sadness is blue,
I hate violence,
And so should you.

So listen to these words,
And you will see,
We are all equal,
And that's how it should be.

When I look a you,
And when you look at me,
Friendly is how it should be.

So let all your grudges go,
And let the kind side of you show,
So all the world knows,
Just how it goes.

Anger is red,
Jealousy is green,
Sadness is blue,
And that's the end,
Of our poem to you.

Jodie Fernandez (11) & Louise Flynn (12)
Turin Grove School

Change It's Easy

The world is at one
Why change?
The environment is one
Why change?
Everyone hand in hand
Why change?

The colours are together
Why change . . .
Heaven and Hell are balanced
Why change . . .
People are living happy lives
Why change . . .
Generations are here
Why change . . .

Sunset and sunrise
Can't change . . .
Tornadoes, earthquakes
Can't change . . .
Mother Nature
Can't change . . .
Ethnic background and religion
Can't change

Can change
Together we can
It's easy
Change!
Change
Change
Change!

Cheyanne Tia Noel (11)
Turin Grove School

Black Or White

I love my country,
Love my race,
Every single person
Should be at the same pace.

Black or white,
Who cares what colour,
What really matters,
Is that we're all here together.

Every person should be
Treated the same,
Because all the people in the world,
Share the same fame.

Black or white,
Who cares what kind,
It's really about what's
In the mind.

I have black friends
And white friends too
I treat them equal,
Because I like them all.

Russell Razzak (12)
Turin Grove School

Domestic Violence

I ran home from school, my mum's black and blue.
I suppose my dad did this to you.
Tears rolling down her face
I think my dad is a total disgrace.
I should have come home earlier
Your hair is no more curlier
Your face is damaged which can't be replaced,
But if I kiss it, it will turn into a smiley face.

Dillon Bakrania (11)
Turin Grove School

Think!

Think!
Of all the people less fortunate than you
Think!
Of all the children who cannot go to school
Think!
Don't waste your food
Think!
Then you will be in a good mood.
Think!
Of all the children with no food.
Think!
Or they will be in a bad mood.
Think!
Reduce, reuse, recycle.
Think!
Don't be a fool!

Molly Tyler & Nakeeyah Sayedchane (12)
Turin Grove School

Race

Roses are red, violets are blue,
Doesn't matter if you're black or white
It's only about you.

Roses are red, violets are blue,
How would you feel if it were you,
What would you do?

Roses are red, violets are blue,
Who would treat someone like that,
What if it were you?

Roses are red, violets are blue,
Now we are at peace, it's all about you.

Ozan Suruk (11)
Turin Grove School

137

Race

Race is a great issue
It can be used in good and bad times too.
Back in the day it was horrible I say,
When racial criticism was thought to be OK.
Chinese, Iraqi, black and white,
Should all be in unity with friendships so tight.
We are all the same,
Black, white - either way.
All I'm trying to express
Is that racial unity is the best.
Think about these strong words
And do something to change the world.

Darnell Fergus (12)
Turin Grove School

Wildlife

Listen to the hummingbirds humming in the trees.
Plus the funny little bunny rabbits that love to nibble on the leaves.
And the cute little bumblebees buzzing in their hives.
Also the mischievous cats that have nine lives.
Do you really want to miss out on the beautiful wildlife?
You should treat the wild like it's your child.

Grace Bester (11)
Turin Grove School

21st Century Ballad

Hoodies and baggy pants.
When they come among you you feel smaller than ants.
The world moves away from Sara as the gang gets closer
Thoughts in her head run around faster than a roller coaster.

Sara looks into the future, she sees her name on a polished stone.
She wishes that would happen so she can be left alone.

Stop bullying, stop bullying, she hears in her dream
She wakes up sweating hotter than steam.
She slowly gets ready for school
Memories of days past makes her feel a fool.
Sara walks out slowly, her big brown eyes.
Water tears rush down her face
A tear ran into her mouth, she hated the salty taste.

She limps to her dungeon of fear where bullies were waiting for her.
She realised it was too quick to give up
A beam of confidence inside her body had struck.
But as soon as she reached the grey gate
Her confidence decreased.

They stared at her, their eyes had hate
They didn't want to but they made it bait.
Their big bodies and eyes shot at her but she
Stayed standing like a door like her feet were glued to the floor.

Face to face they stood
Sara said, 'If no one stops this happening I would
Or you will force me to give my life away
And those that make me will sooner or later have to pay . . .'

Jonida Xhauri (12)
Walthamstow School for Girls

My Dream:

I have a dream of rainbows and ponies
Where everything's nice and everything's cosy
But that's just a dream, that's not reality
My dreams are so different from the things I really see
Everywhere you look there's a fight or gun crime
When I walk down the streets I'm scared, so sometimes
I wish I could go home and be in my bed
And dream pretty dreams when I lay down my head
I'd much rather dream than face the real world
The streets aren't that safe for a young foolish girl
But the world isn't as bad as people think
It can be quite beautiful when the sky turns light pink
Or when the flowers bloom in the spring
Or when all the little birds start to sing
See those are the things that I'd like to see
Every single day for the rest of eternity
Nowadays people are living in sin
Can't we just scrunch that and throw it in the bin
I'd rather live with puppies and flowers
And everyone's brave, there are no cowards
So until my dream becomes the world I live in
I guess I have to wait until the sun starts setting
So I can go to my bed and feel safe while I sleep
And hope when I wake up my day will be sweet.

Alicia Gurman (13)
Walthamstow School for Girls

My Mum

My mum is my shining star
So what if she has no car
I am lucky I am here today
Even though I don't get my own way
I will love my mum every day
And plus I get a say
And it is good her birthday is not in May.

She said I was her saviour
She can't say that about her neighbour.
She has made mistakes recently
But she has always been there for me
Even when I'm late for tea.

Teenagers like getting into trouble
But I like to help and always be on the double
Instead of being trapped inside a bubble.
I get a kiss and a hug instead of hiding under a rug.
My mum stays strong when she knows something's wrong.

I love my mum so much
When I am in trouble and such
She says nothing is more important than her children
And that will be me one day.

Zoë Samantha Sainty (12)
Walthamstow School for Girls

I Have A Dream

I have a dream,
That there was a stream,
And it took me to the right path,
It took me to a path where there was no racism,
No more poverty,
No more wars,
No more bullying and more freedom.

Irum Mughal (12)
Walthamstow School for Girls

Rosa Parks

Life would be so different,
If you got off your seat
If you hadn't said to them
'No! I will not stand on my feet!'

One woman
With a dream to change all
To stay proud
And stand tall

You took a stand
And your people held your hand,
Life would be so different
If you hadn't had a dream

'Equality, freedom and no poverty!'
Is what we all dreamt
We are all the same, so there's no one to blame
Just for the colour of our skin

Racism, gone and definitely history,
Your courage and your strength
That is why you are such an inspiration to me,
Now I have a dream, to beat poverty!

Rahma Mohammed (13)
Walthamstow School for Girls

Harriet Tubman

Freedom is the most important issue to me.
Everyone should be free of slavery.
No more hard working for children and old people.
No more hard life for them and no mistreating.
There will be no slavery.
That's why freedom is the most important thing to me.

Aranee Thurirajah (12)
Walthamstow School for Girls

What Are We Without A Dream?

What are we without a dream?
Lost souls with no goals or aspirations
What are we without a dream?
Lost souls travelling to the wrong destinations
What are we without a dream?
Without a dream you're me
A child unsure of what she desires to be
An actress, chef, musician or architect
I am the fortress of the future I protect
What are we without a dream?
Is the question that I was able to redeem
I may be a child unsure of what she desires to be
But one thing's for sure I will succeed
I will succeed in whatever the future holds for me
My dream is to be an inspiration
That helps someone realise their true aspiration.
Many children across the world don't have a dream
Children like me who aren't sure how they want their life to be
But sooner or later everything will become clear
Today, tomorrow, or maybe even next year.

Keisha Brome (13)
Walthamstow School for Girls

The Bully Ballad

When she wakes up early in the morning,
Without smiling, without yawning.
With a scary image in her head, which makes her wish she
was dead.
Then she leaves her house, and did she have breakfast?
Nope! Leaving at home all her dreams and hopes!
When she enters school sorrowfully, she gets ready to meet her
destiny.
At registration enters her nightmare, with long black hair.
She walks up to her grinning, all the students start cheering.
They all crowd around standing there without sound.
She pulls out a pen knife and flicks her hair.
Everybody watching, they don't care.
She tries to run but there's *no way out!*
All she can do is scream and shout!
At lunchtime she curls up into a ball in a corner.
She has no friends, she's a loner.
Hiding her red spine-shivering marks, all she can do is weep and cry.
Wishing that death is nearby.

Anisa Narot (12)
Walthamstow School for Girls

I Have A Dream

I have a dream
That I won't have to scavenge in the street
Search for food under cinema seats
Won't be beaten day after day
Named and shamed by my dear Uncle Ray
Have a life free from my room
My day's crammed cleaning with that old broom
Be able to wallow in my own muck
Have my very own monster truck
But it's unlikely I'll ever be blessed with the gift
Unless the circles of life have a sudden shift
My little story doesn't add up to much
Held under strict rules with a firm clutch
But it's better like this than it is for some
Beaten and abused 'til they're numb
I guess, my life as a cockroach it isn't that bad
Not like the little boy by the gutter, so sad.

Ronan McKenzie (14)
Walthamstow School for Girls

Young Writers Information

We hope you have enjoyed reading this
book - and that you will continue to enjoy it
in the coming years.

If you like reading and writing poetry drop
us a line, or give us a call, and we'll send
you a free information pack.

Alternatively if you would like to order further
copies of this book or any of our other titles,
then please give us a call or log onto our
website at www.youngwriters.co.uk

Young Writers Information
Remus House
Coltsfoot Drive
Peterborough
PE2 9JX
(01733) 890066